Actes du XIVème Congrès UISPP, Université de Liège, Belgique, 2-8 septembre 2001

Acts of the XIVth UISPP Congress, University of Liège, Belgium, 2-8 September 2001

SECTION 16

PRÉHISTOIRE DE L'ASIE ET DE L'OCÉANIE
ASIAN AND OCEANIC PREHISTORY

Sessions générales et posters
General Sessions and Posters

Édité par / Edited by

Le Secrétariat du Congrès

Président de la Section 16 : Charles Frank Herman

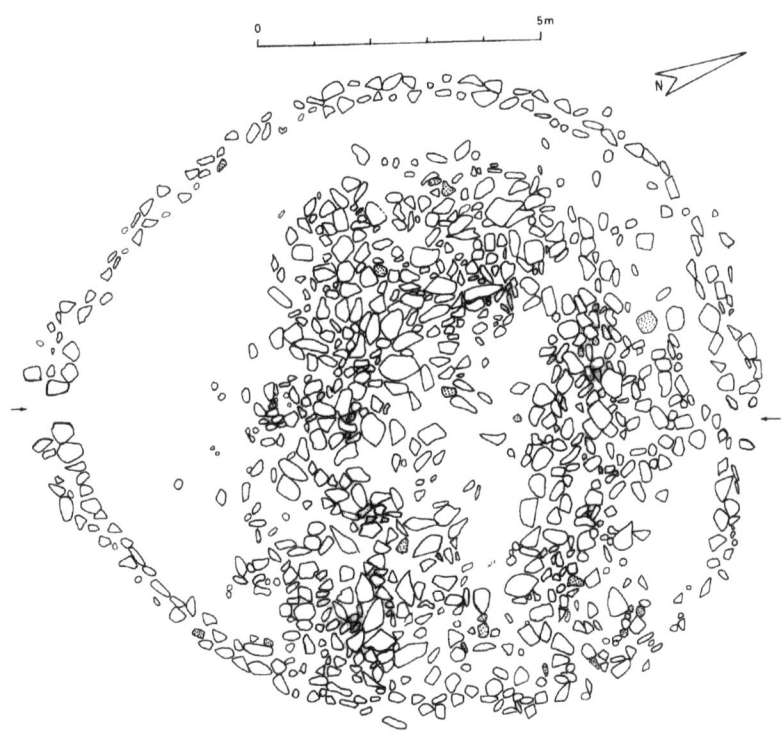

BAR International Series 1523
2006

Published in 2016 by
BAR Publishing, Oxford

BAR International Series 1523

Proceedings of the XIV World Congress of the IUPPS
Actes du XIV Congrès Mondial de l'UISPP

Préhistoire de l'Asie et de l'Océanie / Asian and Oceanic Prehistory

ISBN 978 1 84171 960 3

© UISPP / IUPPS and the editors and contributors severally and the Publisher 2006

Avec la collaboration du Ministère de la Région Wallonne
Direction générale de l'Aménagement du territoire, du Logement et du Patrimoine
Subvention n° 05/13532

Marcel Otte, Secrétaire général du XIVème Congrès de l'U.I.S.P.P.
Université de Liège, Service de Préhistoire, 7, place du XX août, bât. A1, 4000 Liège, Belgique
Tél. 0032/4/366.53.41   Fax 0032/4/366.55.51   Email : prehist@ulg.ac.be
Web : http://www.ulg.ac.be/prehist

Editing : Rebecca Miller
Typesetting and layout: Darko Jerko

The authors' moral rights under the 1988 UK Copyright,
Designs and Patents Act are hereby expressly asserted.

All rights reserved. No part of this work may be copied, reproduced, stored,
sold, distributed, scanned, saved in any form of digital format or transmitted
in any form digitally, without the written permission of the Publisher.

BAR Publishing is the trading name of British Archaeological Reports (Oxford) Ltd.
British Archaeological Reports was first incorporated in 1974 to publish the BAR
Series, International and British. In 1992 Hadrian Books Ltd became part of the BAR
group. This volume was originally published by Archaeopress in conjunction with
British Archaeological Reports (Oxford) Ltd / Hadrian Books Ltd, the Series principal
publisher, in 2006. This present volume is published by BAR Publishing, 2016.

Printed in England

BAR titles are available from:

        BAR Publishing
        122 Banbury Rd, Oxford, OX2 7BP, UK
EMAIL info@barpublishing.com
PHONE +44 (0)1865 310431
FAX +44 (0)1865 316916
        www.barpublishing.com

TABLE DES MATIÈRES / TABLE OF CONTENTS

SESSION GÉNÉRALE / GENERAL SESSION 16-I

Circular Earthworks in East Cambodia and South Vietnam:
  New Results from 2000-2001 1
M.N. Haidle

Niveaux d'habitat et sépultures de l'âge du Fer à Ban Yang Thong Tai,
  province de Chiang-Mai (Thaïlande) 7
J.-P. Pautreau, P. Mornais, T. Doy Asa

Unexplored Valleys, Potential Frozen Kurgans and Heritage Management.
  Belgian Archaeological Research in the Altai Republic
  (Russian Federation): Survey and Inventory 1996-2000 17
I. Bourgeois, J. Bourgeois

Ancient Hunter-Gatherers, First Sedentary Farmers and Nomad
  Stock Herders of Mongolia (8000-3000 BC): New Researches
  at Tamsagbulag (Dornod Aimak) 25
M.L. Séfériadès

Skeletal Markers of Task Activities in Iron Age Human Remains
  from Tell Mishrife (Central Syria) 41
A. Canci, D. Morandi Bonacossi

Le premier peuplement de la Nouvelle-Caledonie : Poteries Lapita
  et sociétés océaniennes colonisatrices 47
C. Sand, J. Bole & A. Ouetcho

Structure, Spatial Metaphors and Landscape: A Study of the Ceremonial
  Marae Temple Grounds in the Society Islands, French Polynesia 53
P. Wallin, R. Solsvik

An Early Iron Age Population Settlement System in Western Siberia 59
N.P. Matveeva

CIRCULAR EARTHWORKS IN EAST CAMBODIA AND SOUTH VIETNAM: NEW RESULTS FROM 2000-2001

Miriam Noël HAIDLE

Résumé : Le groupe homogène des redoutes circulaires à l'Est du Cambodge et au Sud du Vietnam fut mentionné pour la première fois par Louis Malleret en 1959. Au Cambodge, depuis 1996 plusieurs équipes internationales ont intensifié leurs recherches sur ces structures composées d'un mur extérieur et d'un fossé intérieur. L'équipe germano-cambodgienne du Centre d'archéologie de Memot en coopération avec l'Université royale des Beaux-Arts de Pnom Penh ainsi que des maîtres de conférence de l'office allemand d'échanges universitaires (DAAD) concentrent leurs efforts d'investigation d'une part sur la découverte et la localisation de sites qui ne sont pas documentés jusqu'alors, et d'autre part sur les fouilles de sites sélectionnés, à savoir les sites de Krek 52/62, Phoum Beng, Groslier, Trobek et Huoch. En 2000 et 2001 plusieurs nouveaux sites furent étudiés pour leur structure (par ex.: diamètre extérieur de 110-440 m, principalement une ou deux entrées avec différents modèles de construction) ainsi que pour leur situation locale et régionale. Les fouilles effectuées conduisent à interpréter les redoutes comme des villages de riziculteurs caractérisés par un outillage lithique et une production de céramiques locaux. Il n'a pas été possible de prouver que les redoutes aient pu servir dans un but défensif ou comme réservoir d'eau. Bien qu'on ait pas encore trouvé de pièces de métal dans les inventaires des artéfacts excavés des redoutes – probablement en raison des conditions très acides du sol-, cinq fragments d'anneaux en verre provenant de Krek 52/62 de coupe transversale triangulaire voire pentagonale renvoient à la fin d'un complexe culturel du Mimotien de l'âge du fer dans la seconde moitié du premier millénaire AC. Les investigations et les fouilles continueront en hiver et au printemps 2002.

Abstract: The homogeneous site group of circular earthworks in East Cambodia and South Vietnam was first mentioned by Louis Malleret in 1959. In Cambodia, the research on structures with an outer wall and inner ditch has been intensified by several international groups since 1996. The Cambodian-German team of the Memot Centre for Archaeology, in co-operation with the Royal University of Fine Arts, Phnom Penh and lecturers of the German Academic Exchange Service (DAAD), focuses on surveys to find and map yet undocumented sites and on excavating in selected sites, namely Krek 52/62, Phoum Beng, Groslier site, Trobek and Huoch. In 2000 and 2001 several new sites were studied regarding their structure (e.g. outer diameter 110-440 m, one or two entrances with different construction patterns) as well as their local and regional situation. Excavations support the interpretation of the earthworks as villages of rice farmers, with local stone tool and pottery production. A defensive or water storage purpose for the earthen structures could not be proven. Although no metal artefacts have yet been found within the earthworks' artefact inventories – probably due to very acidic soil conditions –, five fragments of glass bangles with triangular to house-shaped cross sections from Krek 52/62 point to an end of the Mimotien cultural complex in Iron Age times in the second half of the first millennium BC. Surveys and excavations will continue in the winter and spring of 2002.

INTRODUCTION

The results presented here are the fruits of a German long-term teaching project at the Royal University of Fine Arts, Phnom Penh, Cambodia directed by Gerd Albrecht (Haidle *et al*. 2001). Field-schools at circular earthwork sites in Eastern Cambodia, analyses of the finds and scientific, as well as popular, presentations of the results are part of the programme which started in 1996 and has since been financed by the German Academic Exchange Service DAAD. In 1999, the first generation with special training in prehistoric field archaeology graduated at the RUFA (Chhor et al. 1999; Heang 1999; Heng & Som 1999; Heng & Mao 1999; Sok & Vin 1999; Thuy 1999) with some of the students now continuing their work on circular earthworks at, or in co-operation with, the Memot Centre for Archaeology. The Memot Centre is a Cambodian scientific project for prehistoric research, management of, and public education on, local cultural heritage of the Ponhea Krek and Memot districts, Kampong Cham Province. The project is kindly supported by the Memot district, the Ministry of Culture and Fine Arts, Phnom Penh, the Krek Rubber Plantation, private German donors, the German Embassy, Phnom Penh, and the German Academic Exchange Service.

CIRCULAR EARTHWORKS IN CAMBODIA AND VIETNAM

Following a small note (Anonymous 1930) the homogeneous site group of circular earthworks in the red soil area of East Cambodia and South Vietnam (Fig. 1) was first mentioned in more detail by Louis Malleret in 1959. With the help of rubber plantation managers he gathered evidence of 17 earthworks, twelve in Vietnam and five in Cambodia. Because of their circular structure with wall and ditch and surface finds of potsherds and polished stone tools, the sites were classified as Neolithic fortresses. In 1962 Bernar Philippe Groslier excavated one of the cir-cular earthworks which he also interpreted as a defensive structure. His reports, only few lines long, are about fourteen cultural layers within a 3 m high stratigraphy. On the basis of the stone artefacts and pottery he found, Groslier defined a new Neolithic culture, the Mimotien (Groslier 1966a, b).

While, in Vietnam circular earthworks have continuously been studied since the 1980s (Luong 1985; Nguyen 1984, 1997, 1999; Nguyen 1986; Pham 1996), knowledge on Cambodian sites has only been increasing for a short time. Since 1996, research on structures with an outer wall and inner ditch in Cambodia has been intensified by several

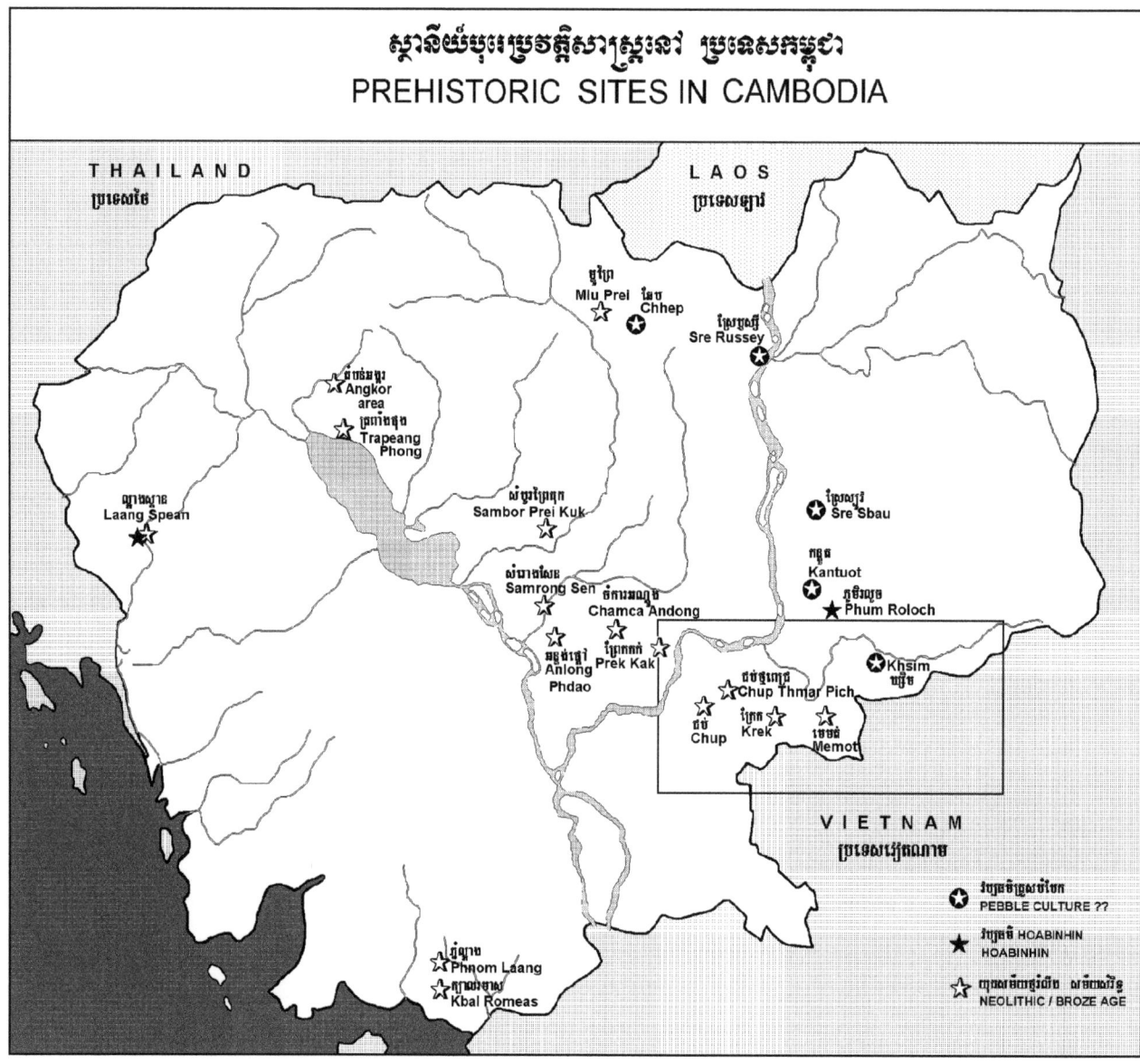

Figure 1. Prehistoric sites in Cambodia. The rectangle marks the distribution area of Mimotien circular earthworks.

international groups (Albrecht & Haidle 1999; Dega 1999, 2002; Kojo & Peng 1997, 1998). The Cambodian-German team of the Memot Centre for Archaeology, in co-operation with the Royal University of Fine Arts, Phnom Penh, has focused on surveys to find and map yet undocumented sites and on excavating in selected sites (Albrecht *et al.* 2001), namely Krek 52/62, Phoum Beng, Groslier site, Trobek and Huoch. In summer 2001, a total of 45 sites were registered, 16 in Vietnam and 29 in Kampong Cham Province, Cambodia (Haidle 2002). As far as is evidenced today, the circular earthworks are restricted to the red laterite soil areas and are mainly situated on slight slopes in elevated areas. Water is accessible in distances between some hundreds of metres and two kilometres (Albrecht *et al.* 2001).

THE LAYOUT OF THE STRUCTURES

Regarding their construction, the analysed earthworks constitute a rather homogeneous site group. The structures are composed of an outer wall and an inner ditch surrounding an inner plateau (Fig. 2). Predominantly, the outer diameter of the earthworks ranges between 200 and 260 m, with a width of between ca. 110 m and more than 440 m. The profiles reveal a common character of the structures which is counterproductive to defensive purposes: the slightly rising outer walls which fall steeply into wide and shallow inner ditches give easy access for attackers. Even if the ramparts had been topped by palisades, the populations inside the structures would have been trapped. As the earthworks are generally built on slight slopes, the ditches are also not capable of storing water for long periods.

Generally, Mimotien circular earthworks possess one single or two opposing entrances generally characterised by depressions in the outer wall. Only Trobek, which is also exceptional in its huge diameter of ca. 440 m and its location near swampy lowlands, shows up to five entrances. For the orientation of the passage no principle preference is detectable. Six different groups of entrance forms have been observed so far (Fig. 3):

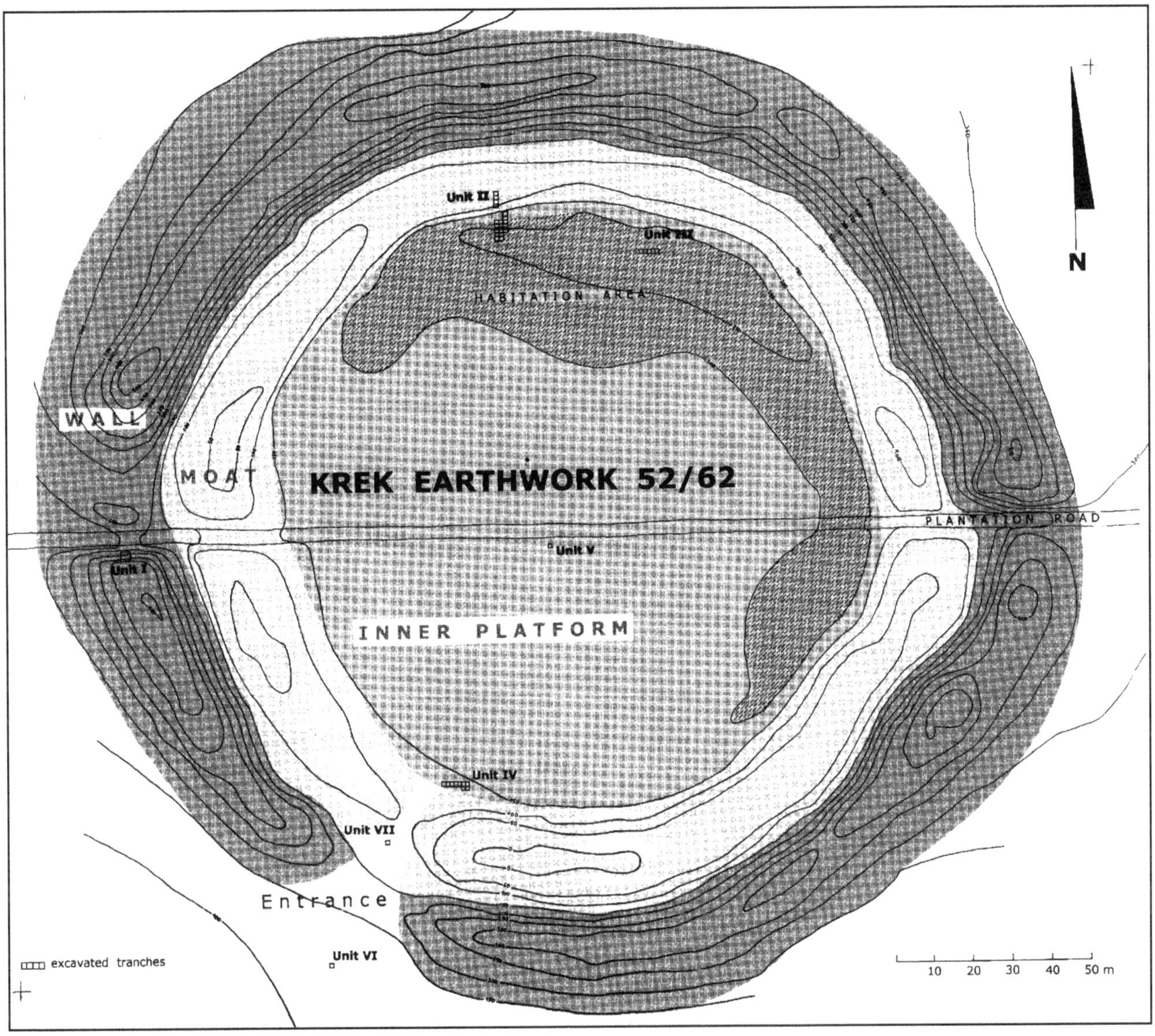

Figure 2. Circular earthwork Krek 52/62, Ponhea Krek District, Kampong Cham Province.

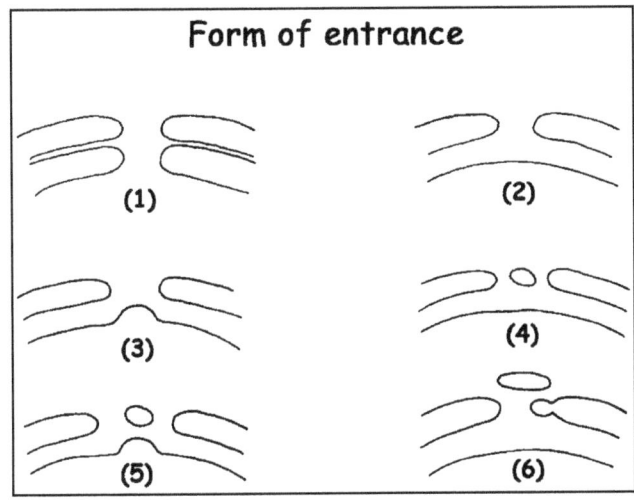

Figure 3. Entrance forms of Mimotien circular earthworks.

1. simple with land bridge: Here the trench is interrupted by the causeway.

2. simple without land bridge: In this variant the trench surrounds the inner plateau throughout.

3. complex with tongue-shaped extension of the inner plateau: This type is characterised by semicircular, to nearly rectangular, earthen annexes of the inner plateau projecting into the ditch.

4. complex with mound: Between the wall terminals a mound was constructed.

5. complex with tongue-shaped extension and mound: The pattern is a combination of types 3 and 4. Semi-circular, to nearly rectangular, earthen annexes of the inner plateau project into the ditch, pointing to a mound between the wall terminals.

6. complex with outer mound: Outside the circular earthworks an elongated mound was built in front of the wall passage. However, this pattern has only been documented once at the circular earthworks Chi Peang.

It can be assumed, that at least the complex structures, were combined with additional bridge constructions of organic material, which has not been preserved. There is no correlation between the form of the entrances and their direction.

Excavations at Krek 52/62 and testpits at several other earthworks including Groslier's site showed the cultural layers concentrating at the edge of the inner plateaux, forming the so called inner embankments. These are not consciously constructed elements but accumulations of potsherds, debris of stone tool production, and broken and rejected artefacts. At Krek 52/62 'pits' were discovered in the occupational layers, containing complete vessels nested together and other artefacts such as spindle whorls. These finds were lying up to 20 cm below the normal finds distribution in the sterile soil (Albrecht et al. 2001; Sok & Vin 1999). Their position within the stratigraphy, however, and with this the relative chronology of their layout within the formation of the archaeological layers, remain unclear. The 'pits' can only partly be demarcated from the surroundings, as all the sediment – sterile, in pits, occupational remains – are homogeneously stained in the dark red colour of tropical laterite soils. In the centre of the inner plateau only a few scattered finds were documented. Contrary to Groslier who mentioned 14 different cultural layers we were able to detect only one or two main strata which might eventually be divided into a few more sub-layers through careful stratigraphic finds analyses.

MIMOTIEN ARTEFACTS

High acidity and increased decomposition rates in the tropical laterite soils result in an impoverished artefact spectrum. No organic material has been preserved, neither bones nor plant fragments, except for impressions and small charred parts of rice grains and husks within the burnt pottery matrix. These traces, however, give evidence for common rice farming near the sites. Both ceramic and stone artefacts are heavily affected by weathering – a lot of fine surface details, traces of the production process or decoration are destroyed. If bronze or iron artefacts had been present at circular earthworks, they would have been completely dissolved at a pH level of the sediment below 4 as it is documented for Krek 52/62 and other sites.

Typical Mimotien pottery was tempered with mineral and/or organic admixture, such as rice husks, and fired at low temperatures. It reveals thin to medium wall thickness characteristic of paddle and anvil technique, also evidenced by a ceramic anvil found at Krek 52/62. On some potsherds remains of a slip are preserved which was combined with various incised, indented, and impressed (cord marked) decoration types. Few pieces show added rims or ornamental bands. Generally, the ceramic ware shows similar forms of vessels and rims as well as decorative styles, but local production can be identified in detail differences, and some special forms such as footed bowls from Krek 52/62 (Chhor et al. 1999; Heng & Som 1999; Heng 1999). Ceramic spindle whorls indicate the production of fabric (Albrecht et al. 2001).

The stone artefact assemblages from the Mimotien circular earthworks (Heng & Mao 1999; Thuy 1999) are composed of knapped and polished adzes which occur in shouldered and butted types. Chisels, probably used for wood-working, a few pointed artefacts and some borers where produced out of the same raw-material, amphibole-hornfels (Neumann 1999). Fresh, then dark grey hornfels, a dense, hard and very fine-grained rock which obtains fairly good properties in processing and use, is available in the region. In a few cases volcanic andesite, silex and quartzite pebbles were used as raw materials for blades, bifacially flaked tools and chopping tools. Another type of stone artefacts is represented by polishing, grinding and whet stones made from fine-grained sandstone. The stone artefacts were produced at the sites: all production stages such as flakes, debris and roughouts are present. Lithophones are also part of the lithic inventory of circular earthworks: fragments are known of from Groslier's excavation and Phu Mieng (Malleret # 8) in adjacent Vietnam.

Different types of ornaments have been recorded from Mimotien circular earthwork sites. Polished stone bracelets have apparently been made from the same metamorphic raw material (hornfels) as chisels and adzes. They show either a flat triangular or a small rectangular cross-section and were manufactured at the sites as production waste proofs. At Krek 52/62 a garnet bead was found. The natural form of the stone with nearly triangular cross-section was maintained: it was simply perforated with double-conical drilling.

Since there are no metal artefacts reported from Mimotien contexts, the discovery of five fragments of five glass bracelets at Krek 52/62 is very exciting. They are made of light and dark green to blue-green translucent glass and reveal a flat triangular to house-shaped cross-section. The chemical composition of the bracelets points to an origin of the glass mass in India or South Vietnam. Except for one, all the glass has soda as a main flux with a minor portion of potash. They show low contents of lime (CaO 1.65-3.06 %) and only traces of barium. Characteristic for the glass* from Krek are * very high values of alumina (Al_2O_3 6.78-7.75 %) (Haidle 2002). Unlike the stone artefacts, which show intensive weathering caused by the acidic soil, the glass fragments are very well preserved, due to their very high alumina contents (Brill 1987).

THE DATING OF THE MIMOTIEN COMPLEX

So far radiocarbon dating of the organic temper of the pottery has not yielded reliable results (Albrecht et al. 2001; Haidle 2002). Other organic material, as well as bronze or iron artefacts, has not been preserved due to the acidity of the red tropical soil with a pH value below 4. These circumstances make the glass bangles highly valuable for dating of the Mimotien earthworks for which different but mainly Neolithic datings were proposed in the past (Fig. 4; cf. Haidle 2002).

Glass was introduced in Southeast Asia in the second half of the first millennium BC (Glover & Henderson 1995). Parallel finds of green to blue translucent glass bangles

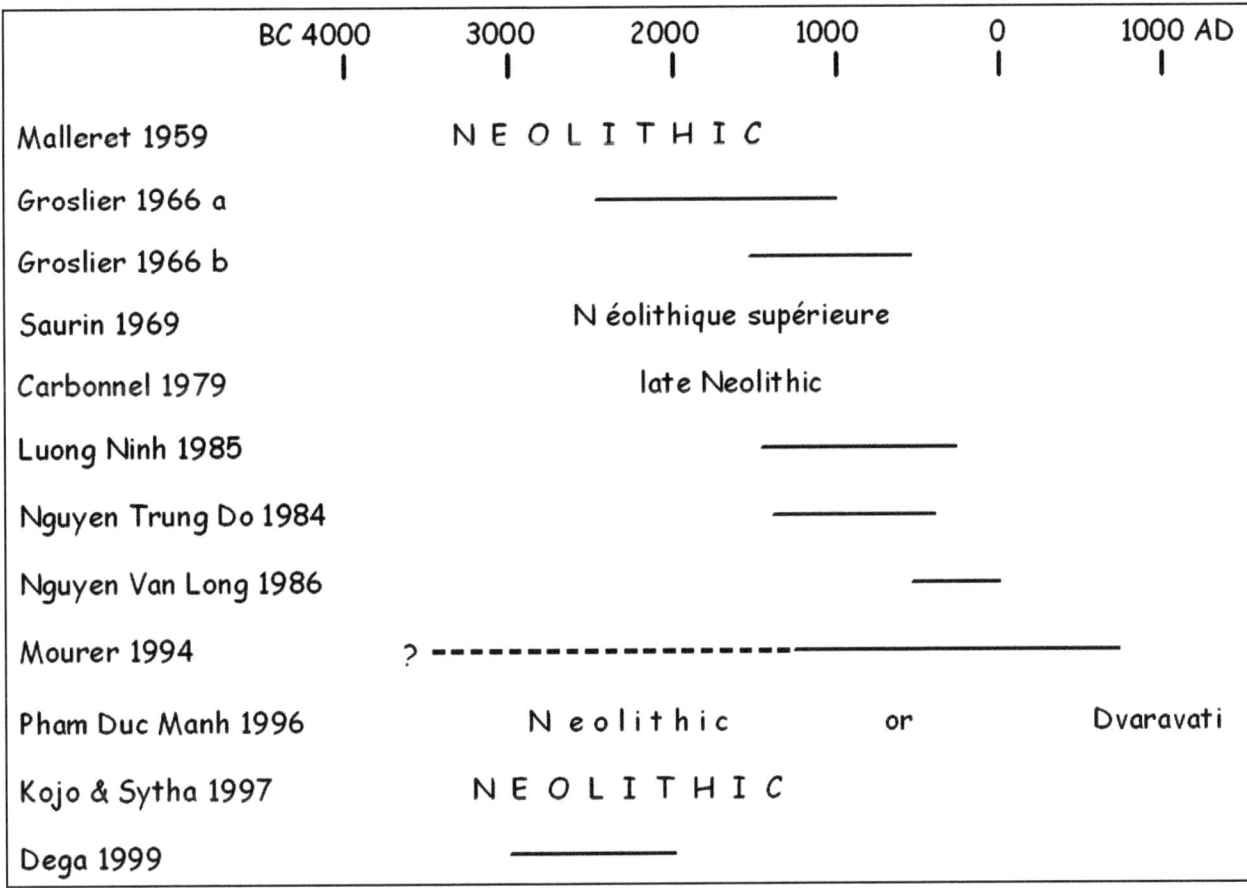

Figure 4. Proposed dating of the Mimotien by different authors.

with triangular to house-shaped cross sections from Vietnam, Thailand and the Philippines date to the second half of the first millennium BC. This characteristic bangle form is typically found in Sa Huynh contexts or with Sa Huynh associated artefacts. Several glass bangles with triangular cross section in dark green, black and violet are reported e.g. from the possible glass production and jar burial site of Giong Ca Vo near Ho Chi Minh City (Francis 1995; cf. Haidle 2002).

The bangle fragments from Krek were all found in the uppermost part, but well within the occupational layer.

This indicates a dating of at least the terminal phase of the Mimotien complex to 500 BC or even younger.

CONCLUSIONS

Excavations support the interpretation of the earthworks as villages of rice farmers with local stone tool and pottery production. A defensive purpose for the earthen structures could not be proven. Although no metal artefacts have yet been found within the earthworks' artefact inventories – probably due to very acidic soil conditions –, fragments of glass bangles from Krek 52/62 point to an end of the Mimotien cultural complex in Iron Age times in the second half of the first millennium BC. Surveys and excavations will continue in the winter and spring of 2002.

Acknowledgments

The research, the results of which I presented here, was generously supported by the German Academic Exchange Service DAAD and the Ministry of Science and Research of Baden-Württemberg. I feel special gratitude for Gerd and Barbara Albrecht, our former students, now colleagues at the Royal University of Fine Arts, Phnom Penh and the Memot Centre for Archaeology, Heng Sophady, Sirik Kada, Thuy Chanthourn and Vin Laychour as well as for Andreas Reinecke, Ian Glover, Peter Francis, Udo Neumann, Nguyen Trung Do, the late Yasushi Kojo and Michael Dega who all were open for fruitful discussions and the share of ideas and data.

Author's Address

Dr. Miriam Noël HAIDLE
Institut für Ur- und Frühgeschichte und Archäologie des Mittelalters
Abt. Ältere Urgeschichte und Quartärökologie
Schloss, Burgsteige 11
D-72070 Tübingen GERMANY
miriam.haidle@uni-tuebingen.de

Bibliography

ALBRECHT, G. & HAIDLE, M.N., 1999, Im Schatten von Angkor Vat? *Archäologie in Deutschland* 3/99, p. 14-19.

ALBRECHT, G., HAIDLE, M.N.; CHHOR, S., HEANG L.H., HENG S., HENG T., MAO S., SIRIK K., SOM S., THUY C. & VIN L., 2001, Circular earthworks Krek 52/62: Recent research on the prehistory of Cambodia. *Asian Perspectives* 39/1-2, 2000, p. 20-46.

ANONYMOUS, 1930, Chronique: Cochinchine. *Bulletin de l'École Française de l'Extrême Orient* XXX/2, p. 576-577.

BRILL, R.H., 1987, Chemical analyses of some early Indian glasses. In *Archaeometry of glass:*, edited by H. C. Bhardwaj. XIV International Congress on glass 1986, New Delhi, India. Calcutta: Indian Ceramic Society, Central Glass and Ceramic Research Institute, p. 1-25.

CHHOR, S., KADA S. & UN T., 1999, *Beng circular earthworks*. Unpubl. final thesis, Faculty of Archaeology, Royal University of Fine Arts, Phnom Penh.

DEGA, M.F., 1999, Circular settlements within Eastern Cambodia. *Bulletin of the Indo-Pacific Prehistory Association* 18, p. 181-190.

DEGA, M.F., 2002, *Prehistoric Circular Earthworks of Cambodia*. BAR International Series. S1041.

FRANCIS, P. Jr., 1995, Beads in Vietnam: an initial report. The Margaretologist 8/2, p. 3-9.

GLOVER, I. & HENDERSON, J., 1995, Early glass in South East Asia and China. In *South East Asia and China: Art, interaction and commerce*, edited by R. Scott & J. Guy. Colloquies on Art and Archaeology in Asia No. 17. London: Percival David Foundation of Chinese Art, University of London, p. 141-170.

GROSLIER, B.P., 1966a, *Archaeologia mundi: Indochine*. Geneva: Nagel.

GROSLIER, B.P., 1966b, Découvertes archéologiques récentes au Cambodge. *Kambuja* 2/16, p. 76-81.

HAIDLE, M.N., 2002, Fragments of glass bangles from Krek 52/62 and their implications for the dating of the Mimotien culture. *Asian Perspectives* 40/2, 2001, p.

HAIDLE, M.N., ALBRECHT, G. & ALBRECHT, B., 2001, Ein Anfang vom Ende des Forschung-kolonialismus? Ein Entwicklungshilfeprojekt zum Aufbau einer eigenständigen Feldarchäologie in Kambodscha. *Archäologische Informationen* 23/1, p. 99-108.

HEANG, L.H., 1999, *The pottery from Groslier circular earthworks site, stored in the National Museum Phnom Penh*. Unpubl. final thesis, Faculty of Archaeology, Royal University of Fine Arts, Phnom Penh.

HENG, S., & SOM, S., 1999, *Analysis of pottery from circular earthworks Krek 52/62*. Unpubl. final thesis, Faculty of Archaeology, Royal University of Fine Arts, Phnom Penh.

HENG, T. & MAO, S., 1999, *Study of stone tools from circular earthworks Krek 52/62*. Unpubl. final thesis, Faculty of Archaeology, Royal University of Fine Arts, Phnom Penh.

KOJO, Y. & PENG, S., 1997, A newly discovered earthwork in Southeastern Cambodia. *Anthropological Science* 105/3, p. 181-187.

KOJO, Y. & PENG, S., 1998, A preliminary investigation of a circular earthwork at Krek, Southeastern Cambodia. *Anthropological Science* 106/3, p. 229-244.

LUONG Ninh, 1985, Circular earthworks. *Khao Co Hoc* 1985/3 (in Vietnamese).

MALLERET, L., 1959, Ouvrages circulaires en terre dans l'Indochine Méridionale. *Bulletin de l'École Française de l'Extrême Orient* XLIX, p. 409-434.

NEUMANN, U., 1999, *Raw material of the stone artefacts from circular earthworks in Kampong Cham province, Cambodia and in S- Vietnam*. Paper presented at the Conference on 'Circular earthworks in Cambodia', 14-19 November 1999, Phnom Penh.

NGUYEN Trung Do, 1984, *Loc Ninh circular earthwork. In Oc-eo culture and ancient culture in the Mekong Delta*. Long Xuyen publishing house (in Vietnamese).

NGUYEN Trung Do, 1997, Problems of research on Bhin Phuoc circular earthworks. In *Archaeological problems in the South of Vietnam*. Social Sciences Publishing House (in Vietnamese).

NGUYEN Trung Do, 1999, Circular earthworks in Binphuoc province. Paper presented at the Conference on 'Circular earthworks in Cambodia', 14-19 November 1999, Phnom Penh.

NGUYEN Van Long, 1986, Circular earthworks in Song Be province. *Khao Co Hoc* 1986 (in Vietnamese).

PHAM Duc Manh, 1996, Proto-history and pre-history of the Eastern part of Nam Bo – past and modern perceptions. *Vietnamese Studies* 1996/2, Special: Archaeological Data II, New Series 50 (120), p. 63-119.

SOK, K. & VIN L., 1999, *Stratigraphy and settlement pattern of circular earthworks Krek 52/62*. Unpubl. final thesis, Faculty of Archaeology, Royal University of Fine Arts, Phnom Penh.

THUY, C., 1999, *Groslier circular earthworks site in Memot District. The stone tools in the National Museum Phnom Penh*. Unpubl. final thesis, Faculty of Archaeology, Royal University of Fine Arts, Phnom Penh.

NIVEAUX D'HABITAT ET SEPULTURES DE L'AGE DU FER À BAN YANG THONG TAI, PROVINCE DE CHIANG MAI (THAILANDE)

Jean-Pierre PAUTREAU, Patricia MORNAIS & Tasana DOY ASA

Résumé : Le site Ban Yang Thong Tai, près du Doi Saket, province de Chiang Mai (Thaïlande) a livré des sépultures attribuées à l'âge du Fer et des niveaux d'habitat des périodes protohistoriques et historiques.

Abstract: In the site of Ban Yang Thong Tai, near Doi Saket, Chiang Mai's province (Thailand) were excavated graves dated from Iron age and settlement levels from protohistoric and historical periods.

L'évolution culturelle des premières civilisations agricoles et métallurgiques des grands bassins alluviaux du nord de la Thaïlande reste particulièrement mal connue, au contraire du Nord-Est du pays et de la vaste plaine centrale de la Chao Praya. On a longtemps cru que cette région de moyenne montagne et de piémont était restée à l'écart des mouvements qui animent à la fin du dernier millénaire avant notre ère les grandes plaines propices à la riziculture. Des recherches menées à Ban Yang Thong Tai, dans la vallée de la rivière Kwang, affluent de la Ping ont livré des documents intéressants.

SITUATION

Le site (thombol de San Pu Lei, amphur de Doi Saket) est à 10 km au nord-est de Chiang Mai. Il correspond au village actuel de Ban Yang Thong Tai (village du grand arbre doré, sud), sur la terrasse de la rivière Kwang, affluent de la Ping (latitude 18° 48' 45" nord, longitude 99° 05' 42" est). De nos jours, c'est un petit relief où les alluvions anciennes (horizons Lampang/Sansai, un sédiment de type humique grisâtre) dominent d'un mètre les rizières environnantes. Il occupe une aire mesurant environ 500 m sur 250 m.

La région présente une topographie peu accidentée de bassin alluvial. Elle est dominée au sud-ouest par une série de collines dont l'altitude est légèrement supérieure à 800 m (Doi Pui, Doi Suthep), plus près le Doi Saket domine de quelques dizaines de mètres la plaine. L'environnement végétal est caractérisé par une forêt de futaie ouverte sur les hauteurs. Dans les terres basses où se trouve le gisement, le paysage naturel de savane a disparu devant une mise en culture généralisée sous forme de rizières et de vergers.

HISTORIQUE

En 1986, à l'occasion du creusement d'un bassin piscicole, dans la partie sud-ouest du village on a découvert un squelette accompagné de bracelets, d'une épée et de poteries. L'inventeur a aussitôt prévenu la division d'Archéologie du *Fine Arts Department*. Les archéologues de Chiang Mai, sous la responsabilité de M. Sayan Prischanchit, ouvrirent, en avril et mai 1986, un sondage près du lieu de la trouvaille (Prischanchit, 1988). Ces travaux ont permis la mise au jour d'une nouvelle sépulture accompagnés d'un intéressant mobilier. En 1999 d'autres recherches, menées dans le cadre du *Thai French Prehistoric Research Project*,[1] ont entraîné, avec l'ouverture de 4 sondages, la découverte de niveaux d'habitat, de dépôts et d'une nouvelle inhumation. Les découvertes sont déposées au Musée national de Chiang Mai ; une partie est exposée.

LES NIVEAUX D'HABITAT

Trois des sondages de 24 m^2 réalisés au printemps 1999 ont livré des vestiges d'une occupation ancienne des lieux. **Le sondage n°1** a été implanté dans la partie centrale du léger tertre correspondant au village actuel.

Stratigraphie : Le sol naturel est atteint à environ 1,60 m au-dessous de la surface actuelle de circulation. Les sédiments denses et compacts proviennent de dépôts alluviaux, gris clair à jaunâtre, contenant un grand nombre de nodules ferrugineux. L'observation des sections permet de distinguer 5 horizons principaux. Le niveau supérieur 4 (10 cm à 40 cm d'épaisseur), un sédiment gris, correspond au sol actuel. Le niveau 3 (20 cm à 30 cm d'épaisseur) est un sédiment très sableux variant du blanc au beige. Il est traversé par de nombreuses racines (l'arbre géant ayant donné son nom au village est à une quinzaine de mètres). Le secteur ouest du sondage contient de nombreux tessons de céramiques historiques lanna (culture du nord) provenant en grande partie des ateliers et fours de San Kampaeng (mortiers, pots, lampes…, fig. 3, n°8, 9, 10, 13) et aussi des fragments de céramiques chinoises (bleus glaçurés, fig. 3, n°1-4). La partie est du sondage, a livré des ossements fragmentaires et en mauvais état. Il pourrait s'agir des restes d'un buffle d'eau. Le niveau 2 (40 cm à 90

---

[1] L'équipe de terrain, sous la direction de J.-P. Pautreau (CNRS, Mission archéologique française) et Tasana Doy-Asa (Fine Arts Department), avec P. Mornais (AFAN, Mission archéologique française) responsable de l'Anthropologie de terrain, était constituée de V. Mariuz et P. Rocas (étudiants en archéologie à l'Université de Poitiers), de Wanchai Chaitep, Tunkaew Khamrapich, Baochan Khamrapich, Wilai, Wait, Lek (fouilleurs permanents), de Areeya Boonplaung (traductions) et de plusieurs ouvriers temporaires.

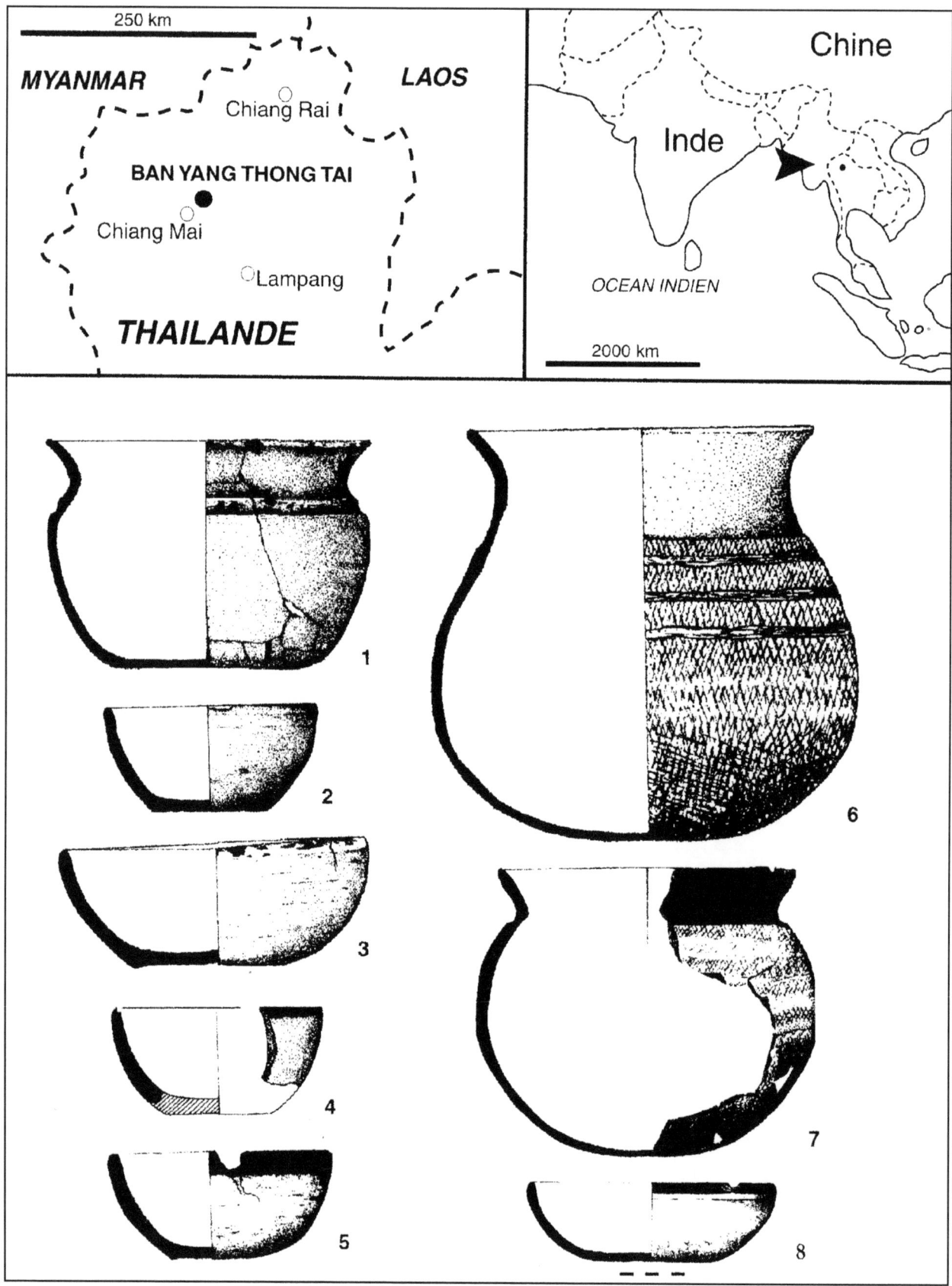

Figure 1. Ban Yang Thong Tai. Situation. Céramiques des sépultures de 1986. Sépulture de la découverte : 5 à 8. Sépulture du sondage : 1 à 4 (*d'après Prischanchit 1988*).

cm d'épaisseur) correspond à un horizon argileux de couleur jaune dans la moitié est de la fouille et à un dépôt sableux pulvérulent dans la zone occidentale. A sa partie inférieure, cette couche comporte de très nombreuses inclusions de fer et de manganèse. C'est à la base de ce niveau que reposent des poteries, façonnées à la main et

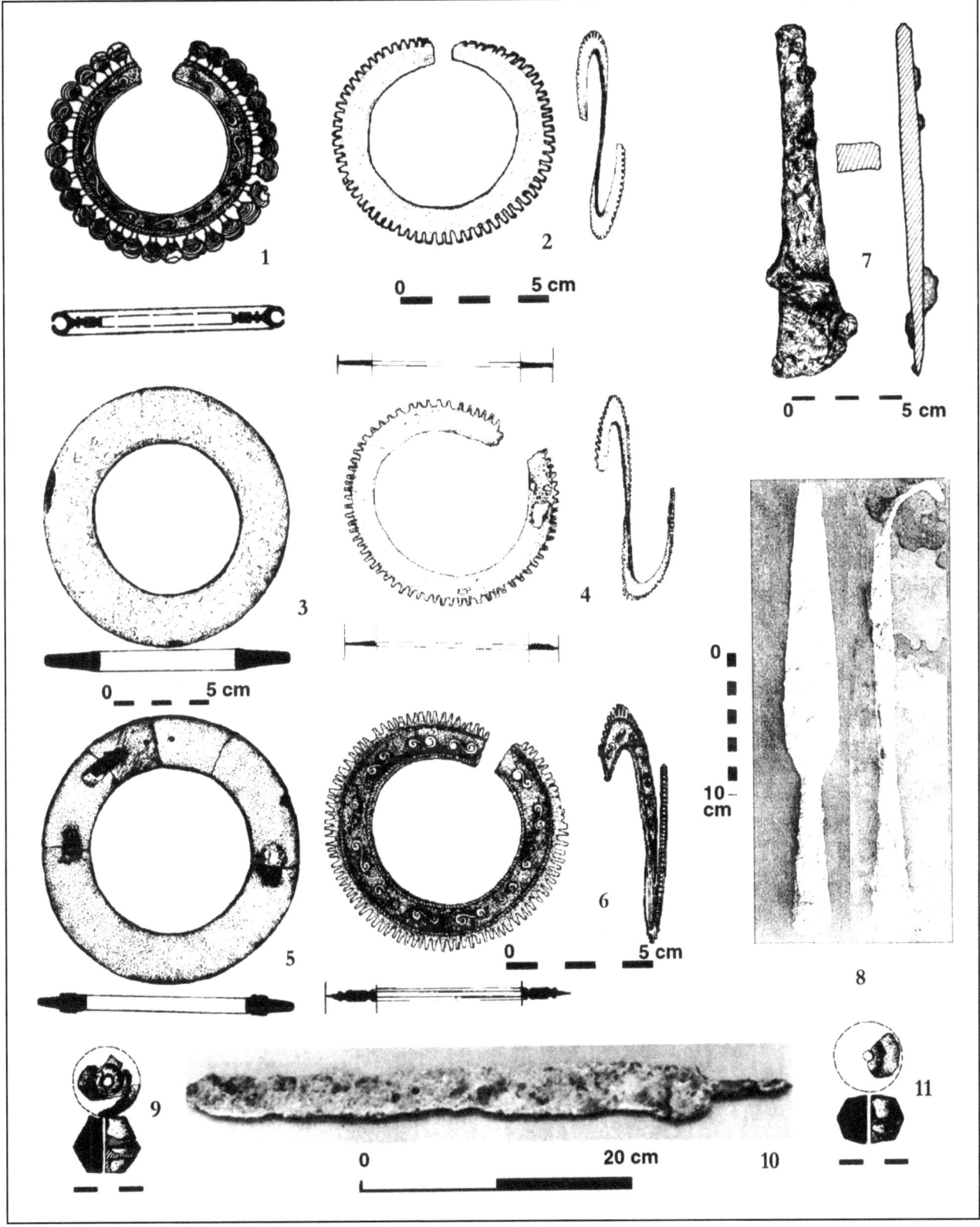

Figure 2. Ban Yang Thong Tai. Parures et mobilier métallique des sépultures de 1986. Sépulture de la découverte : 3, 5, 10. Sépulture du sondage : 1, 2, 4, 6, 7 à 9, 11 (d'après Prischanchit 1988).

cuites sous meule, caractéristiques de la protohistoire locale.

- un récipient à fond plat portant un épaulement marqué à la base du col (fig. 4, n°4) a été retrouvé brisé en un grand nombre de tessons. Des traces de peinture rouge ont été observées sur la lèvre. Diamètre à l'ouverture : 221 mm. Diamètre du fond : 178 mm. Hauteur : environ 214 mm.

- un vase à fond arrondi muni d'un court col éversé (fig. 4, n°2). Diamètre à l'ouverture : 140 mm. Diamètre

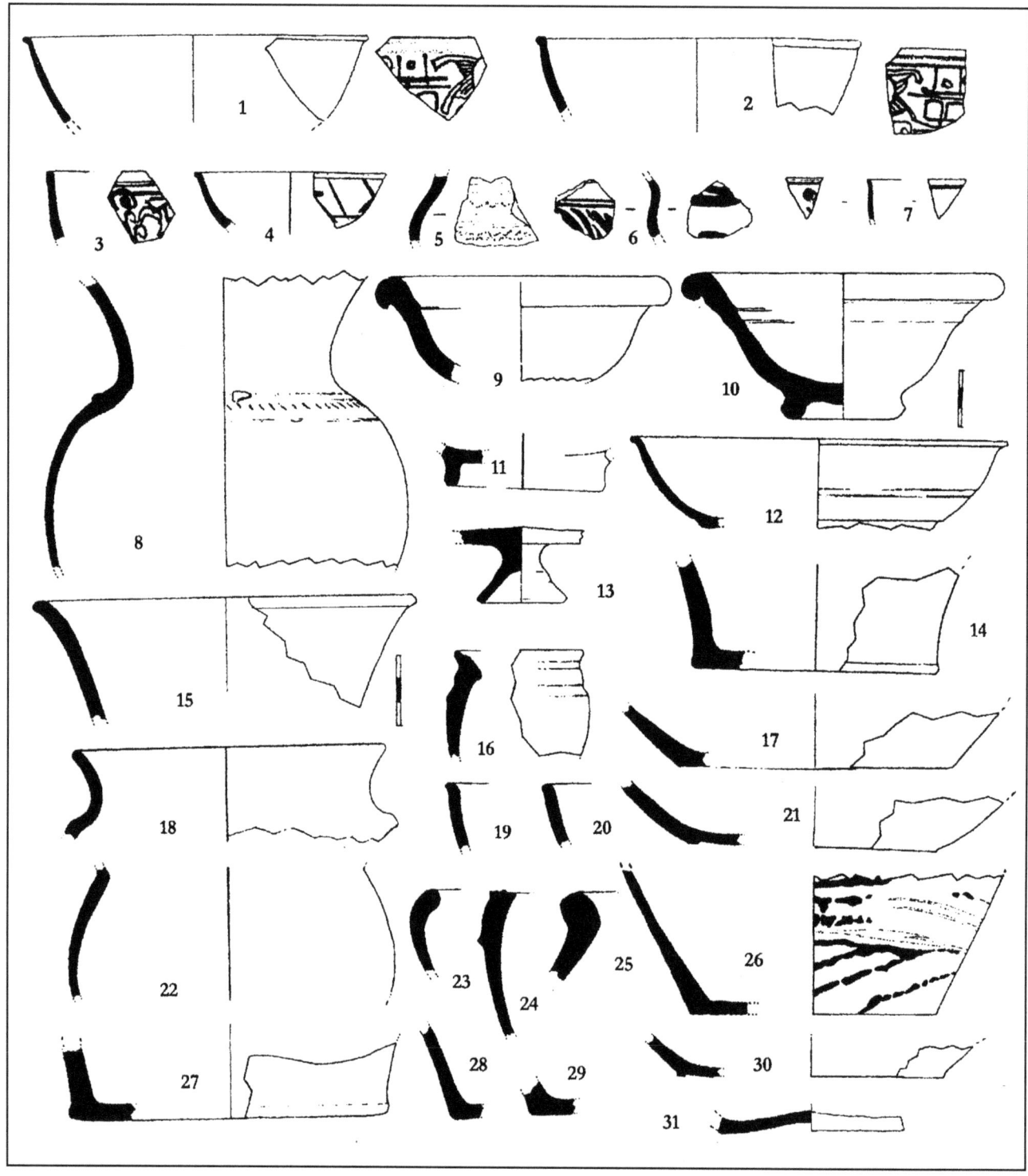

Figure 3. Ban Yang Thong Tai. Céramiques des niveaux historiques (*dessins M.A.F.T., V. Mariuz, P. Rocas*).

maximum : environ 200 mm. Hauteur : 150 mm. Traces d'impressions.

- un vase à court col éversé. Diamètre à l'ouverture : environ 125 mm. Traces d'impressions (fig. 4, n°3). Ces deux derniers vases étaient disposés dans une même fosse, associés à un outil en fer très corrodé.

Le niveau 1, inférieur (20 cm à 45 cm d'épaisseur) est un sédiment argileux à dominante brun foncé -mais la couleur de cet horizon peut varier du gris au noir- comportant de nombreuses inclusions ferrugineuses. Dans la zone ouest, il est remplacé par un sable compact. Il contenait une structure de petites pierres de 80 cm de diamètre ayant subi l'action de la chaleur. Cet aménagement peut correspondre aux vestiges d'un foyer préhistorique. Une partition apparaît entre le secteur ouest sableux et la zone est argileuse, ceci indépendamment des horizons archéologiques. Elle est bien visible sur l'ensemble des coupes. Cette différence sédimentaire peut s'expliquer par la présence de chenaux et de bassins comblés.

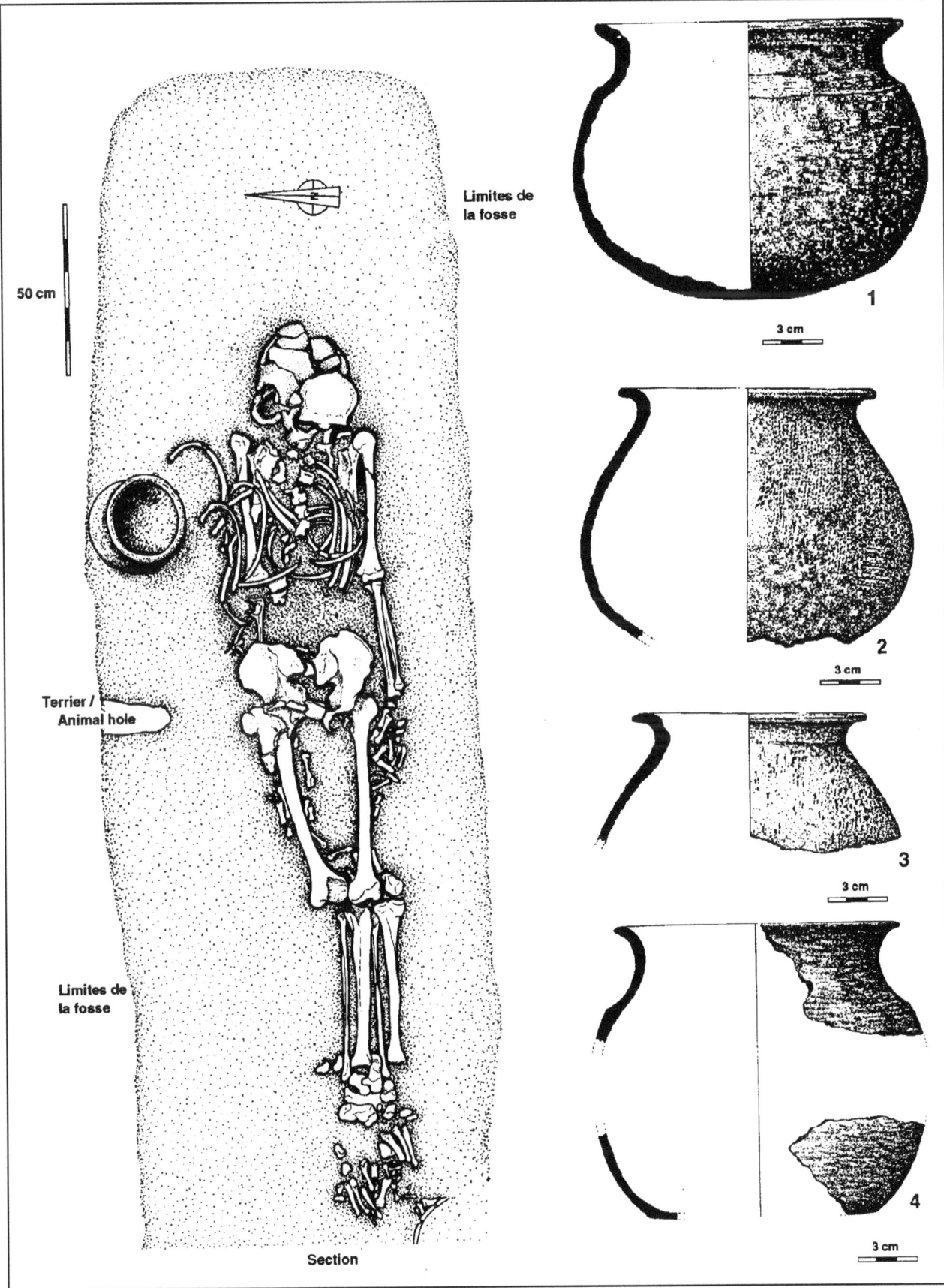

Figure 4. Ban Yang Thong Tai. Sépulture de 1999 : plan, céramique : 1. Sondage n°1 de 1999 : céramiques protohistoriques : 2 à 4 (*relevé et dessins M.A.F.T., P. Mornais*).

Le sondage n°2 a été ouvert dans le secteur ouest à proximité des rizières, à environ 60 m à l'ouest de la fouille précédente. La stratigraphie est identique à celle du sondage n°1. Le sol naturel a été atteint à environ 1,10 m au dessous de la surface actuelle de circulation. Dans la couche 3, au sédiment argileux pulvérulent,. un foyer avec une aire d'argile rubéfiée a été mis en évidence au nord-est du sondage, à la base du niveau. Un dépôt cendreux est visible dans la section Est. L'horizon suivant renferme un petit nombre de tessons pré ou protohistoriques à l'ouest et du centre du sondage. Le sol naturel est constitué par des alluvions sableuses.

Le sondage n°3, en bordure sud-ouest du village, à seulement 2 m de l'emplacement des trouvailles de 1986, montre un sédiment absolument similaire à celui observé dans les autres sondages. Le sol naturel, vierge, apparaît à une profondeur voisine de 1,20 m à 1,40 m. La couche n°2 est composée d'un sédiment argilo-sableux beige ou d'une argile jaunâtre. La partie supérieure renferme des nodules ferrugineux. Dans le secteur sud-est, le fond de cette couche est traversé par 3 trous de poteaux. L'un d'eux est contemporain, les deux autres sont historiques. Les artefacts issus de ce niveau (céramiques chinoises, tessons Hariphunchai) invitent à une datation historique. Dans la partie nord-est du sondage la base du niveau 2 est constituée par un horizon plus jaune. C'est cet horizon, si l'on se réfère aux observations de 1986, qui correspond au sol pré-protohistorique des inhumations. Ici, à 2 m des deux sépultures, il ne contient pas le moindre vestige.

LES SEPULTURES

Les sépultures de 1986

La sépulture de la découverte a été mise au jour à environ 80 cm de la surface actuelle du sol (Prischanchit, 1988, p. 72-74). Les restes osseux recueillis (fragments crâniens, vertèbres, côtes, clavicules, scapula, pelvis, os longs des membres supérieurs et inférieurs, phalanges) bien que brisés et fragmentaires permettent aux archéologues du *Fine Arts Department* de proposer une détermination sexuelle (masculin), un âge (50 à 55 ans) et une stature (aux alentours de 1,70 m).

Le mobilier d'accompagnement

▸ Les céramiques. Toutes sont façonnées sans usage du tour.

– Un récipient globulaire à fond arrondi, court col éversé à lèvre arrondie (fig. 1, n°6). Passage panse-col en "S" adouci. La panse porte des incisions et des empreintes de battoir. La partie supérieure de la panse est ornée par trois lignes d'incisions parallèles. Hauteur : 35 cm, diamètre à l'ouverture : env. 31,5 cm, diamètre de la panse : env. 36 cm. Pâte brun foncé, surfaces rosées, dégraissant sableux (Prischanchit, 1988, p. 75).

– Un récipient globulaire, panse quasi sphérique, court col éversé à lèvre arrondie (fig. 1, n°7). Jonction panse-col anguleuse. La panse porte des incisions recouvertes de traces de battoir. Le col est peint en rouge foncé (hématite ?) à l'extérieur comme à l'intérieur. Hauteur : environ 17 cm, diamètre de la panse : env. 20 cm. Pâte brun gris. (Prischanchit, 1988, p. 76).

– Une écuelle à fond plat ou aplati, paroi concave, très court bord sub-vertical prolongeant la paroi (fig. 1, n°8). Hauteur : 6,5 cm, diamètre à l'ouverture : 18,5 cm, diamètre à la base : 10 cm, épaisseur moyenne des parois, 0,6 cm. Pâte noire à l'intérieur, rosé à l'extérieur, surface rose à jaune, dégraissant sableux. La lèvre est peinte en rouge foncé (extérieur comme intérieur), (Prischanchit, 1988, p. 77).

– Une écuelle à fond plat, paroi concave, pas de bord véritable, la lèvre arrondie prolonge la paroi (fig. 1, n°5). Hauteur : 5,2 cm, diamètre à l'ouverture : 11,1 cm, diamètre à la base : 4,3 cm. Pâte gris foncé à rosé, surface gris foncé. Lèvre peinte en rouge foncé (extérieur et intérieur), (Prischanchit, 1988, p. 77).

– Les fragments d'un grand récipient portant des traces d'empreintes de battoir (Prischanchit, 1988, p. 76).

▸ Les parures. Il s'agit de deux bracelets en marbre blanc. Le premier mesure 13, 09 cm de diamètre (fig. 2, n°3). L'autre, brisé anciennement en 4 fragments conserve les traces de réparations avec des fils de fer (fig. 2, n°5), (Prischanchit, 1988, p. 76 à 78).

▸ Un seul objet métallique. Une épée en fer à soie longue et étroite ; l'extrémité est brisée (fig. 2, n°10). Longueur : 45,5 cm, largeur de la lame : 4,2 cm (Prischanchit, 1988, p. 78).

La sépulture du sondage du *Fine Arts Department*. L'inhumation individuelle a été mise au jour à environ 80 cm de profondeur à proximité immédiate de la précédente. Le squelette semble perturbé anciennement (plan in Prischanchit, 1988, p. 94-95). Il est orienté tête à l'Est. L'examen du pelvis invite les fouilleurs à proposer une détermination sexuelle (féminin). L'âge attribué est de 30 à 35 ans et la stature avancée est d'environ 1,50 m. (Prischanchit, 1988, p. 90-95).

Le mobilier d'accompagnement

▸ Les céramiques. Toutes sont façonnées sans usage du tour.

– Un récipient à fond aplati ou plat, paroi évasée, col court, bord éversé à lèvre arrondie (fig. 1, n°1). Déposé aux pieds du défunt. Cannelure horizontale à la base du col. Traces de battoir sur le fond. Traces de peinture rouge sur les rebords externe et interne. Hauteur : 12,5 cm, diamètre à l'ouverture : env. 18,1 cm, diamètre de la panse : env. 18 cm. Pâte gris à rose (Prischanchit, 1988, p. 100-101).

– Un bol ou écuelle à fond légèrement concave, lèvre arrondie prolongeant la paroi évasée (fig. 1, n°3). Déposé à gauche du défunt, en bordure de la tombe, pas très loin des objets métalliques. Traces de peinture rouge sur le rebord externe et interne. Hauteur : 6,2 cm, diamètre à l'ouverture : env. 18,6 cm, diamètre du fond : env. 9,5 cm. Dégraissant sableux, surface gris à rose (Prischanchit, 1988, p. 98-99).

– Un bol ou écuelle à fond légèrement plat, lèvre arrondie prolongeant la paroi évasée (fig. 1, n°2). Déposé aux pieds du défunt avec le premier vase décrit. Traces de peinture rouge sur les rebords externe et interne. Hauteur : 5,2 cm, diamètre à l'ouverture : env. 11 cm, diamètre du fond : env. 6 cm. Pâte similaire au précédent (Prischanchit, 1988, p. 100).

– Fragments du col et du haut de la panse d'un grand récipient plus ou moins pansu, col concave marqué, bord éversé à lèvre arrondie. La panse porte des incisions croisées et des empreintes de battoir. Elle est ornée par deux groupes de deux lignes d'incisions parallèles. L'extérieur de la base du col au rebord et l'intérieur de la lèvre sont peints en rouge (Prischanchit 1988, p. 101). Fragments du col et du haut de la panse d'un récipient de taille moyenne plus ou moins pansu, bord éversé épaissi à lèvre arrondie. La panse porte des incisions croisées et des empreintes de battoir et trois lignes d'incisions parallèles. L'extérieur, de la base du court col au rebord, et l'intérieur de la lèvre sont peints en rouge. (Prischanchit 1988, p. 101). Fragments du col et du haut de la panse d'un récipient de taille moyenne plus ou moins pansu, col court marqué, long bord éversé à lèvre arrondie. La panse porte des incisions croisées et des empreintes de battoir et cinq lignes d'incisions parallèles. L'extérieur, de la base du court col au rebord, et l'intérieur de la lèvre sont peints en rouge. Diamètre oral autour de 24 cm (Prischanchit 1988, p. 101).

– Un bol ou écuelle à lèvre arrondie prolongeant la paroi évasée (fig. 1, n°4). Peinture rouge sur le rebord externe et interne. Hauteur : env. 5,5 cm, diamètre à l'ouverture : env. 11 cm. Pâte similaire à celle des autres bols (Prischanchit, 1988, p. 102).

– Les tessons d'un récipient globulaire à fond rond de taille moyenne. Empreinte cordées obtenues au battoir. Les tessons d'un vase à fond rond. Empreintes cordées obtenues au battoir, peinture rouge. Les tessons d'un petit bol avec peinture rouge sur le rebord interne et externe Prischanchit, 1988, p. 98).

▸ Deux fusaïoles brisées, la première (fig. 2, n° 11). Diamètre : env. 3 cm, hauteur : 2 cm, l'autre (fig. 2, n° 9). Diamètre : env. 3 cm, hauteur : 2,8 cm.

▸ L'outillage métallique. Une pointe de lance à douille en fer (fig. 2, n° 8), trouvée près du fémur droit. Extrémité ployée. Longueur : 30 cm, largeur de la flamme : 4 cm. Une lame du type "ciseau" ou "hache" (fig. 2, n°7), trouvée près du fémur droit, partiellement sur la pointe de lance. Tranchant étroit légèrement arqué, zone d'emmanchement épaisse à section rectangulaire. Longueur : 15,8 cm, largeur au tranchant : 3,4 cm.

▸ Les parures. Un bracelet circulaire ouvert en métal base cuivre, jonc à section triangulaire (fig. 2, n°6) trouvé près du fémur droit, partiellement sous la pointe de lance. La bordure extérieure est dentée. Le plat du jonc porte une ligne de 12 motifs en "S" horizontaux en relief, encadrée par deux lignes de grènetis évoquant une cordelette. Diamètre : 8,05 cm, largeur du jonc : 1,53 cm, épaisseur : 0,14 cm. Un autre similaire (fig. 2, n°6) trouvé près du fémur droit, à côté de la pointe de lance. Le plat du jonc n'est pas décoré. Diamètre : 7,01 cm, largeur du jonc : 1,05 cm, épaisseur : 0,14 cm. Un troisième identique (fig. 2, n°6) trouvé autour de l'avant-bras droit. La bordure extérieure est dentée. Le plat du jonc n'est pas décoré. Diamètre : 7,85 cm, largeur du jonc : 1,27 cm, épaisseur : 0,13 cm.

La sépulture du sondage n°4 de1999. Le sondage n°4 limité à 15 m² mesurait 5 m sur 3 m ; il a été creusé à l'est du village, tout près de la rizière actuelle. Cet emplacement était, lui aussi, cultivé en rizière voici une quarantaine d'années. La stratigraphie est identique à celle observée dans les autres sondages. Dans la partie supérieure de la couche 2 subsistaient quelques tessons de vases avec des traces de peinture rouge sur la lèvre. C'est à partir de ce niveau qu'est apparu l'emplacement d'une sépulture, à environ -1,30m par rapport au sol de circulation actuel. La tombe contient le squelette d'un adulte orienté Est-Ouest, tête à l'Est, accompagné d'un vase globulaire déposé contre lui, à sa droite. Les ossements sont dans un bon état de conservation, mais l'examen limité des coxaux n'a cependant révélé aucun caractère discriminant permettant la détermination sexuelle de l'inhumé. La sépulture a été conservée *in situ,* sans prélèvement des ossements.

La tombe se présente comme une assez vaste fosse quadrangulaire aux angles arrondis : sa largeur est de 0,75m et sa longueur de plus de 2,40m (son extrémité occidentale disparaît dans la paroi du sondage). Une concentration régulière de nodules ferrugineux en dessine assez nettement les contours, tandis que le sédiment de comblement, bien que tout aussi compact que le sédiment encaissant se différencie de ce dernier par une texture plus poudreuse ; l'emploi du marteau et du burin a néanmoins été nécessaire pour le dégagement de la surface des pièces osseuses. Le squelette repose sur le dos, les membres supérieurs étendus et serrés le long du corps, les membres inférieurs allongés. La position d'origine du corps est globalement conservée, mais on remarque cependant plusieurs déplacements d'os (désorganisation des cotes droites, position incohérente du sacrum près du coxal droit, disparition de nombreuses dents...) dont les causes demeurent hypothétiques : bouleversement dû à l'intrusion d'un petit animal (un terrier a été décelé à proximité) ?, violation de la tombe (et dans ce cas, la pauvreté relative de la sépulture n'est peut-être qu'apparente) ?, ou encore simple phénomène taphonomique ? La chute d'un objet lourd et périssable (couvercle de cercueil en bois ?) off-rande déposée dans la tombe ?...) est également envisageable pour expliquer le bouleversement de l'hémithorax droit, mais aussi le roulement latéral des tibias et fibula droite, poussés vers la parois gauche.

En dehors de toute trace du contenant, les seuls indices concernant le mode d'inhumation restent d'ordre taphonomique. Le squelette apparaît légèrement décentré vers la gauche, l'ensemble des membres supérieur et inférieur gauches s'alignant par ailleurs parfaitement le long d'une même paroi rectiligne, disparue, distante d'environ 15cm du bord de la fosse ; on note à cet égard une surélévation de plusieurs centimètres du membre supérieur gauche comprimé par la paroi, par rapport au reste du corps. La contrainte exercée par le contenant disparu est également perceptible à travers la compression générale du squelette, bien nette notamment au niveau des épaules : le squelette occupe un espace plutôt restreint par rapport à la largeur de la fosse, comme si l'inhumé avait été placé dans un contenant un peu étroit.

A l'intérieur de ce contenant, le glissement des os des mains le long des fémurs et le détachement des os des pieds vers l'extrémité de la tombe suivent le pendage général du fond, mais indiquent aussi que la décomposition du corps s'est réalisée dans un espace qui n'a pas été colmaté immédiatement par de la terre : un contenant rigide et étroit, donc, mais aussi relativement étanche, du moins un certain temps. La nature exacte de celui-ci nous échappe pourtant : le corps a t'il été enserré dans un linceul épais à la fois rigide et flexible, de type natte végétale ou linceul en peau, avant d'être déposé dans la fosse avec peut-être davantage de mobilier funéraire qu'il n'en a été retrouvé (les vastes dimensions de la fosse l'y autoriseraient) ? Ou bien l'inhumé a-t-il été déposé dans un véritable cercueil en bois, façonné par exemple dans un tronc d'arbre évidé à l'égal des sépultures de la nécropole protohistorique voisine de Ban Wang Hai (Pautreau, Mornais, Doi-Asa, 2002, p. 21) ? Dans ce cas, les contours de la fosse pourraient en réalité matérialiser les parois externes du cercueil, mais l'emplacement du vase contre la paroi s'avère alors pour le moins énigmatique....

Cette inhumation, accompagnée par une seule poterie, semble relativement pauvre, comparée aux deux sépultures anciennement trouvées à Ban Yang Thong Tai. Le vase est une poterie globulaire montée à la main et cuite sous meule. Elle possède un fond rond, un court col éversé et un épaulement marqué (fig. 4, n°1). Diamètre à l'ouverture : 157 mm. Diamètre maximum : 180 mm. Hauteur : 133 mm. Aucune trace de peinture rouge n'est visible sur le rebord. Le fond porte des incisions et/ou de fines traces d'impressions cordées. La pâte montre une texture très fine et comporte l'ajout d'un dégraissant sableux. Le seul traitement de surface visible consiste en traces de lissage.

REMARQUES GÉNÉRALES

– Le mobilier archéologique protohistorique

Les céramiques constituent les vestiges les plus abondants avec des formes pansues à col évasé au fond plat, aplati ou hémisphérique puis des bols ou écuelles à fond plat. Ces récipients semblent avoir été façonnés à la main, monté au colombin et terminé au battoir. Le "décor" d'impressions de cordes, produit apparemment par un battoir entouré de cordelettes est souvent "sur-incisé" (séries de petites incisions parallèles courtes), et parfois totalement oblitéré par les incisions postérieures concernent quasi exclusivement le fond du vase ou parfois la panse. Les formes corrélées à ces décors sont le plus souvent de vases globulaires à cols éversés. Les cols, en liaison douce ou angulaire, sont souvent lissés, jamais décorés. Le passage col-panse ou la partie supérieure de la panse peut porter des cannelures ou incisions horizontales. Certains cols sont peints en rouge (hématite probablement). Cette forme de céramique est abondamment représentée sur la plupart des sites prospectés ou fouillés en Thaïlande du Nord et dans les contrées voisines, dès le Néolithique. Il apparaît souvent associé à un ou plusieurs types de céramiques mieux caractérisés, ici les petites écuelles à peinture rouge sur le bord. La peinture rouge, utilisée dans le Nord-Est pour décoré des céramiques, n'a pas été retrouvée, en dehors de Ban Yang Thong Tai, dans les rares sites fouillés du Nord.

Les fusaïoles ne se rencontrent que dans les horizons tardifs des sites néolithiques et protohistoriques comme Ban Chiang, Non Pa Kluay or Ban Don Ta Phet (Glover 1990, 175), Ban Wang Hai (Pautreau, Mornais, Doy-Asa 2001, p. 69). Elles semblent associées avec l'utilisation de fibres textiles filées et paraissent caractériser des tâches féminines, même si plusieurs exemples ethnologiques asiatiques montrent la réalisation d'activités de filage par les hommes (Cameron 2000).

La pointe à douille à flamme triangulaire allongée ressemble plus à celles trouvées à Ban Wang Hai (Pautreau, Mornais, Doy-Asa 2001, p. 41) qu'aux exemplaires lancéolés des autres gisements thaïlandais de l'âge du Fer comme Noen U Loke, Ongbah ou Ban Don Ta Phet. Ban Don Ta Phet a produit sept pointes de lance à douille en fer, la plupart sacrifiées par ploiement de la flamme (Glover 1990). Il est difficile de se prononcer sur la mutilation du seul exemplaire recueilli à Ban Yang Thong Tai. La lame en fer du type "hache" ou "ciseau" a été interprétée comme outil aratoire par S. Prischanchit (Prischanchit 1988). La seule autre épée reconnue comme telle en Thaïlande provient d'une sépulture au riche mobilier du site voisin de Ban Wang Hai (Pautreau, Mornais, Doy-Asa 2001, fig. 176b). Au Cambodge, une épée a été retrouvée, également dans une sépulture privilégiée, sur le site de Phun Snay (O'Reilly, Sytha, 2001, p. 265). L'absence d'épée dans la plaine centrale et dans le Nord-Est et, au contraire, le cantonnement des exemplaires connus au Nord, peut être interprété comme une influence des cultures chinoises, probablement sensible, dans la région, à l'âge du Fer. Les épées, à lame de bronze ou de fer, connues dans les cultures du sud de la Chine ou au Viet Nam montrent toutefois des morphologies assez différentes de celles de Thaïlande du Nord.

Pour ce qui est des parures, les bracelets de marbre s'ils sont bien attestés dans le Nord-Est (Ban Na Di ou un exemplaire est cassé et réparé avec un fil de Bronze, Non Praw, Ban Lum Khao) et la plaine centrale (Nong Nor), datent surtout de l'âge du Bronze (Higham, Thosarat p. 101, 112, 115, 121). Les bracelets en bronze, originaux dans leur conception, probablement réalisés à la cire perdue, reproduisent des motifs ornementaux bien attestés dans les horizons tardifs de Ban Chiang et dans plusieurs cultures régionales de l'âge du Fer. Il faut noter l'absence totale de parures en pâte de verre.

– Les sépultures. Les deux sépultures de 1986 peuvent être contemporaines (utilisation du fer, vases à peinture rouge) ; leur contemporanéité avec celle de 1999 n'est pas établie même si la présence de poteries au bord peint en rouge dans le niveau immédiatement supérieur, la rend plausible. La disposition des tombes, tête au S.-E.

pour la tombe fouillée en 1986, E.-N.-E. pour celle de 1999, diffère peu. Cette orientation se retrouve dans plusieurs cimetière du pays même si elle n'est pas dominante. Les 3 personnes inhumées sont des adultes. Les sondages, limités au regard de la superficie du site, donnent toutefois l'impression d'inhumations plus ou moins isolées au sein même du village, plutôt que de sépultures rassemblées en cimetière.

– Les autres découvertes. Les vestiges historiques comportant des tessons de vases vernissés de type San Kampaeng correspondent bien à un niveau d'habitat. Les fours de San Kampaeng ont été en activité entre les 13ème et 17ème siècles de notre ère. La signification des vestiges protohistoriques du sondage 1 de 1999 paraît différente. Les vases sont écrasés en place et ne sont pas accompagnés de tessons isolés. Les deux récipients associés avec un outil en fer, tout comme le vase fragmenté, semblent des dépôts délibérés plutôt que des rejets liés à une activité quotidienne. L'absence de restes funéraires ou de structure domestique à proximité ne permet pas pour autant de leur attribuer une fonction précise, domestique ou autre. La présence de peinture rouge invite à associer ce niveau aux sépultures dégagées en 1986. Celles-ci, de datation incertaine, peuvent avec bien des réserves, être attribuées au début du premier millénaire de notre ère. L'aménagement de pierres brûlées trouvé à la base du niveau inférieur est manifestement antérieur à l'horizon contenant les vases protohistoriques ; aucun vestige ne lui est associé.

Le manque de recherches dans le nord de la Thaïlande et le petit nombre de gisements étudiés, en comparaison avec le Nord-Est et la plaine centrale, ne permettent pas d'attribution culturelle ou chronologique précise. L'absence de collagène dans les os n'a pas permis de datations C14. Dans le bassin de Chiang Mai – Lamphun, les seuls éléments similaires sont la nécropole de Ban Wang Hai, et à un degré moindre le site de Ban Sa Pha Ka et plus loin, dans la vallée de la Mae Chem, la sépulture de Ob Luang. Les découvertes de Ban Yang Thong Tai constituent néanmoins un nouveau jalon, important dans l'établissement de la chronologie des temps pré-protohistoriques dans le nord de la Thaïlande.

Remerciements

Nous remercions la Commission consultative des fouilles archéologiques à l'étranger, M. J.-C. Jacq et Mme F. d'Orgeval à la Sous-Direction des Sciences Sociales et Humaines du Ministère des Affaires Etrangères, Le *National Research Council of Thailand*, le *Fine Arts Department of Thailand* et en particulier, M. Somchai Na Nakorn Phanom, alors Directeur du 6ème bureau régional du Département des Beaux-Arts puis Mme Somsuda Leelayawanich, alors responsable des Musées, Chiang Mai, sans qui notre mission n'aurait pu avoir lieu. Nous avons reçu l'appui des Services Culturels et de Coopération de l'Ambassade de France à Bangkok avec M. J.-C. Terrac, Conseiller et Mme Martine Herlem, Attachée de Coopération et, à Chiang Mai, celui de l'E.F.E.O. avec L. Gabaude et celui de l'Alliance Française en la personne de T. Baude. Que tous trouvent ici l'expression de notre gratitude. Enfin, nous n'oublions pas l'accueil chaleureux réservé par les autorités de Ban Yang Thong Tai : M. Wasan et Mme Ampika Sudachan, le maire et son épouse et par les propriétaires des terrains sondés : Mme Baochan Khamrapich, M. Udom Khamrapich et M. Jankhaw.

Adresses des auteurs

Jean-Pierre PAUTREAU
Directeur de recherches au CNRS, UMR 6566 CNRS
Bât. 25, av. Général Leclerc
35042 Rennes, FRANCE
et
Mission Archéologique Française en Thaïlande
2, rue Saint-Nicolas
86370 Château-Larcher, FRANCE
E-mail : pautreau@club-internet.fr

Patricia MORNAIS
Archéologue AFAN
Collaborateur à l'UMR 6566 du CNRS et Mission Archéologique Française en Thaïlande
18, rue des Trois Rois
86000 Poitiers, FRANCE

Tasana DOY ASA
Archéologue
Research Section
Fine Arts Department
Chiang-Mai Museum
Super Highway
Chiang-Mai THAILAND

Bibliographie

CAMERON, J., 2000, Prehistoric spindlewhorls as cultural markers in Southeast Asia, *8th Intern. Conference, Association of Southeast Asian Archaeologists in Western Europe*, Abbazia di Spineto, Sarteano, Italy, 2-6 october 2000, abstracts.

GLOVER, I., 1990, Ban Don Ta Phet : the 1984-85 excavation, in Ian and Emily Glover édit., *Southeast Asian Archaeology 1986, Proceedings of the First Conference of the Association of Southeast Asian Archaeologists in Western Europe*, Institute of Archaeology, University College London, 8th-10th September 1986, BAR International Series 561, 1990, p. 139-184, 22 fig., Oxford.

HIGHAM, C., THOSARAT, R., 1998, *Prehistoric Thailand, From Early Settlement to Sukhotai*, River Books, 234 p.

O'REILLY, D.-J.-W., SYTHA, P., 2001, Recent excavations in Northwest Cambodia, *Antiquity*, 75, p. 265-266, 3 fig.

PAUTREAU, J.-P., MORNAIS, P., DOI ASA, T. 2000, Iron tools and weapons in Ban Wang Hi necropolis, Lamphun, Northern Thaïland, *8th Intern. Conference, Association of Southeast Asian Archaeologists in Western Europe*, Abbazia di Spineto, Sarteano, Italy, 2-6 october 2000, abstracts, 2 p., 1 fig.

PAUTREAU, J.-P., MORNAIS, P., DOI ASA, T. 2002, *Ban Wang Hai, un cimetière de l'âge du Fer en Thaïlande du Nord*, Silkworm Books.

PRISHANCHIT, S., 1988, Ban Yang Thong Tai, in CHAROEN-WONSA P. édit., *Archéologie du Nord: Muang Mae Moh,*

Obluang, Ban Yang Tong Tai. Publications de la Division de l'Archéologie, Département des Beaux-Arts, Bangkok, B.E. 2531 -EN THAI-.

PRISHANCHIT, S. édit., 1997, *Archaeology in Lanna*, F.A.D., Bangkok, 400 p. -EN THAI-.

SANTONI, M., PAUTREAU, J.-P., et PRISHANCHIT, S., 1990, Excavations at Obluang, Province of Chiang Mai, Thailand, *Southeast Asian Archaeology 1986, Proceedings of the First Conference of the Association of Southeast Asian Archaeologists in Western Europe*, Inst. of Arch., University College London, 8th-10th September 1986, ed. by I. and E. Glover, BAR Int. Series 561, 1990, p. 37-54, 6 fig.

SORENSEN, P., 1973, Prehistoric iron implements from Thailand, *Asian Perspectives*, vol. XVI 2, 1973, p. 134-173.

UNEXPLORED VALLEYS, POTENTIAL FROZEN KURGANS AND HERITAGE MANAGEMENT. BELGIAN ARCHAEOLOGICAL RESEARCH IN THE ALTAI REPUBLIC (RUSSIAN FEDERATION): SURVEY AND INVENTORY 1996-2000

Ignace BOURGEOIS & Jean BOURGEOIS

Résumé : Le Département d'Archéologie et d'Histoire Ancienne de l'Europe (Université de Gand) est depuis 1995 activement engagé dans la recherche archéologique en République d'Altai (Fédération de Russie). Dans un premier temps initié comme un projet centré sur l'étude et la fouille de tombelles (kourganes) scytho-sibériens, le projet fut assez rapidement élargi à la prospection et l'inventarisatio. Au printemps 1996, une prospection permit la localisation et la description de 49 sites, dispersés dans 17 vallées. Une prospection intensive et un inventaire détaillé des vallées de Sebÿstei et de Kalanegir, en 1996 et 1997, mena à la découverte de plus de 350 monuments, surtout des monuments funéraires ou rituels d'époque scytho-sibérienne ou turcque, ainsi que plusieurs centaines de pétroglyphes. La plupart de ceux-ci sont concentrés à des emplacements spécifiques, répondant à un certain ordre. Il est intéressant de mentionner la découverte dans la vallée de Kalanegir, d'une zone à permafrost comptant plusieurs monuments scytho-sibériens. Des recherches similaires ont été menées dans le plateau des steppes d'Ujmont (1999) et dans la région de Maima (2000). Actuellement, le Département d'Archéologie étudie la possibilité d'utiliser les images satellites (CORONA) pour la détection et l'interprétation des structures archéologiques. Il entre dans nos intentions, à partir d'une prospection systématique et d'un inventaire détaillé, avec l'appui des archéologues et géographes locaux, d'aider à la mise en place d'un système de valorisation (et de protection) du patrimoine archéologique de la République d'Altai.

Abstract: From 1995 onwards, the Department of Archaeology and Ancient History of Europe at Ghent University (Belgium) has been actively involved in the archaeological research in the Altai Republic (Russian Federation). What started out as an excavation project on Scytho-Siberian burial mounds (kurgans), was soon widened in scope. Large-scale field surveys became the most important part of the following campaigns. The spring 1996-survey resulted in the mapping and describing of 49 sites in 17 valleys. An intensive survey of the and the valley (1996 and 1997) led to the discovery of more than 350, mostly Scytho-Siberian and Turkic, funeral and ritual monuments and several hundreds of petroglyphs. Most of them are clustered according to a fixed pattern and are built on specific geographical locations. Worth mentioning is the finding of a permafrost zone with Scytho-Siberian kurgans in the Kalanegir valley. Similar investigations were carried out in the Ujmonski steppe (1999) and in the Maima area (2000). Presently, the Department is investigating whether the use of satellite images (CORONA pictures) can be useful in the detection and interpretation of archaeological structures. It is our aim to develop, starting from systematic surveys and the processing of the collected data, a valorisation system for the archaeological heritage of the Republic in co-operation with archaeologists and geographers of the Gorno-Altaisk State University.

INTRODUCTION

The Altai Republic, part of the Russian Federation, is situated in Central Asia at the meeting point of four countries: Mongolia, China, Kazakhstan and the Republic itself (fig. 1). Archaeologically this region (the Altai Mountains) became quite famous since the discovery of the frozen burials at Pazyryk in the middle of last century and the recent finds on the Ukok plateau and at Berel' (see a.o. Rudenko 1970, Derevianko & Molodin 2000 and Samashev e.a. 2000). All of these were dated to the so-called Scytho-Siberian period, situated between the fifth and third century BC.

The history of Belgian archaeological research in the Altai Mountains is rather recent. It started with the exhibition "The Gold of the Scythians" organised in 1991 in the Royal Museums of Art and History in Brussels (Cahen-Delhaye 1991). Immediately after this exhibition, the Royal Museums set up a co-operation with Russian colleagues. Initial research was focused on the excavation of Scytho-Siberian burial mounds, the so-called *kurgans*, in the southern part of the Altai Republic. This resulted in excavation campaigns during the summers of 1992, 1993, 1995 and 1996. From 1995 onwards, an interdisciplinary research programme on the Scytho-Siberian culture started with, amongst others, the Department of Archaeology and Ancient History of Europe at Ghent University (more information in Bourgeois e.a. 2000). This article deals with the surveys that were carried out between 1996 and 2000.

RESEARCH METHOD

The campaigns of 1996 and 1997 led us to the south of the Republic, concentrating on two valleys which were archaeological *terra incognita* at that time. The valleys of the Sebÿstei and the Kalanegir are both situated in the southern part of the Chuya depression. The depression is situated at an altitude of 1800 m.a.s.l. and is surrounded by mountain ranges up to 3900 m.a.s.l. (fig. 2).

Research in these valleys had two complementary directions. Geographical, pedological and geophysical research provided insight into the genesis and the present physical situation of the valleys. Archaeological research aimed at a better understanding of their occupational history. In order to gain this insight, the research consisted in making a detailed inventory of all archaeological monuments and petroglyphs, using a differential global positioning system.

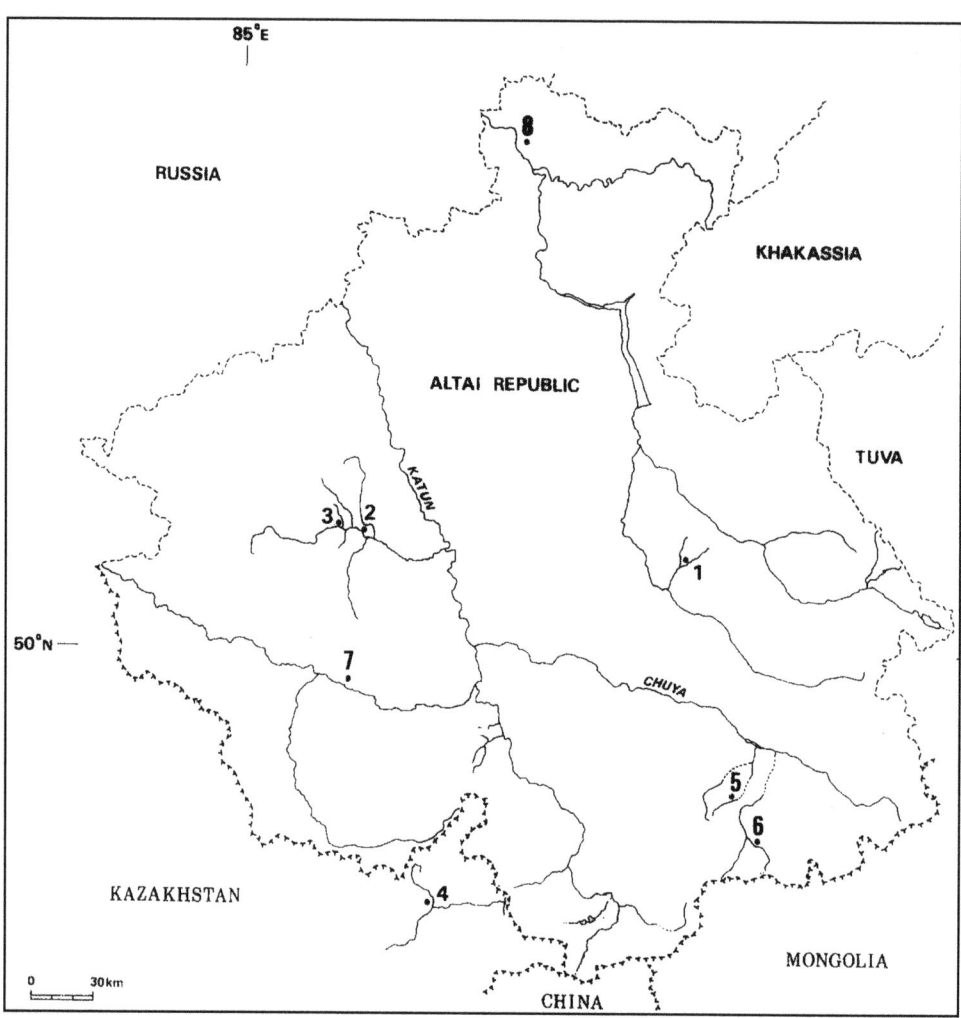

Figure 1. The Altai Republic (1: Pazyryk; 2: Tuekta; 3: Bash Adar; 4: Berel'; 5: Sebÿstei; 6: Kalanegir; 7: Ujmonski steppe; 8: Maima).

The accumulated evidence should provide a good impression of the valleys themselves, their occupational history and their value and importance to past generations. This research method made it possible to situate the valleys in a broader, regional perspective. It should also be emphasised that besides the undeniable scientific value of an interdisciplinary approach, these data are also extremely useful for the management of the archaeological heritage and for the development of an archaeological policy (see e.g. Kubarev 1991 and 1992, Jacobson & Meacham 1998 and Chang e.a. 1999).

SEBŸSTEI VALLEY (1996-1997)

Sebÿstei is one of the smaller, north-south orientated valleys that cut into the South Chuya Range which is the southern border of the Chuya depression. The research was carried out as described above during the summer campaigns of 1996 and 1997 (the data are published *in extensu* in Bourgeois e.a. 1999a).

STRUCTURES - As a result of the survey, more than 300 archaeological structures from different periods were found (fig. 3). They were built on flat or slightly sloping surfaces, spread out over the three main geographical units of the valley: 4 archaeological structures were found in the upper part; 230 structures, almost two out of three, were found on the terraces in the middle part; 88 structures were found in the lower part of the valley which is the flat transition zone to the Chuya depression. All have a clearly funerary or ritual character. With the exception of several recent *zimniki* (winter camps for herdsmen), no remnants of permanent or temporary settlements were discovered.

The occupation of the valley covers a period of at least 4000 years. The oldest structures date from the Bronze Age (end 4th millennium BC - beginning 1st millennium BC). These include eight Afanasiev graves (an Early Bronze Age culture), four steles (large, standing monoliths) and five *kereksurs* (rectangular or circular ritual monuments with occasional small circles of buried stones around them) (fig. 4). The majority of the structures dates from the Scytho-Siberian period (c. 800-200 BC). Two different types occur. The most important group are the kurgans (round small and low cairns). A second type of Scytho-Siberian structures are ritual circles. These monuments can be divided into two subtypes. One type consists of standing stones, the other of buried ones. The standing stones are always found in connection with the kurgans.

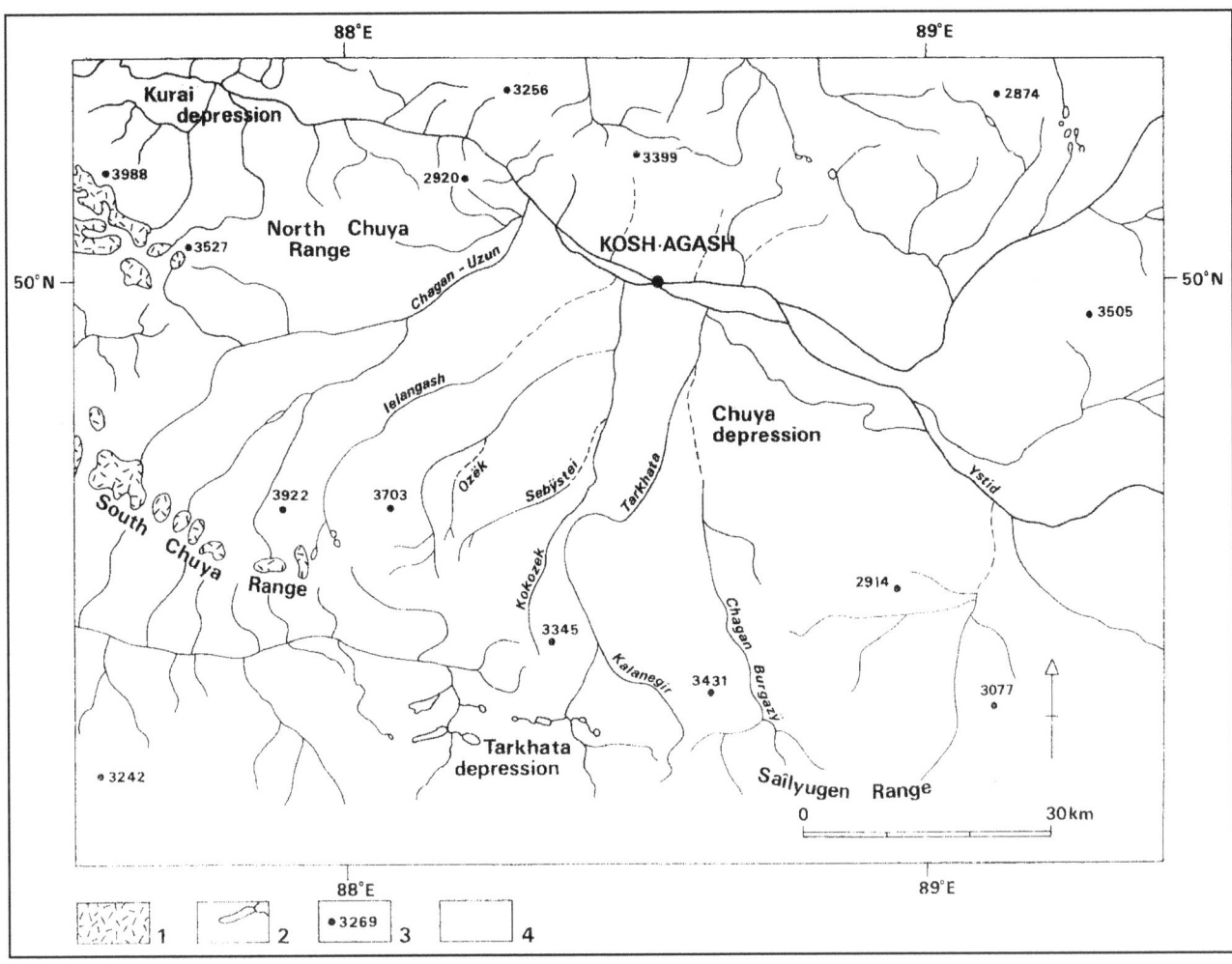

Figure 2. The Chuya depression and adjacent valleys
(1: glacier and firn basins; 2: rivers and lakes; 3: absolute altitudes; 4: depressions).

The buried ones are isolated and scattered over the valley. Only one structure, an oval shaped grave, can be related beyond doubt to the Hunnish period (c. 200 BC - 500 AD). The second most important group of structures dates from the Turkic period (c. 500 - 900 AD). There are two different types: burial mounds and *agradki*. The Turkic burial mounds are also called kurgans. Most of them are solitary monuments. Most Turkic structures are agradki. Their basic form is a small rectangle bordered by schistose slabs buried at their edge. Inside this area, there is a clear accumulation of stones. A *balbal* (standing stone) or a chain of balbals often appears east of an agradka. Four of these balbals are sculptured. They show typical naturalistic or stylised male figures. The so-called Ethnographical period (c. 1750 AD - Russian revolution) is represented by three types of structures. Burial structures are the first one. The second type are small stone heaps. These ritual structures lie scattered over the whole valley, especially at physical "borders". The last type are curved "walls" of heaped stones. Their function is disputable but might be related to cattle breeding.

The main part of the structures (210 monuments, 2/3 of the total) is clustered. In Sebÿstei seventeen clusters can be defined. Eleven of them were built according to the same basic plan: the later structures were built around a Scytho-Siberian core. In the centre, there is a north-south orientated alignment of kurgans. To the west and more or less parallel to the mounds lie one or more ritual circles made of standing stones. Sometimes, a balbal or a chain of balbals was constructed east of the kurgans. Turkic agradki were mainly built east of the Scytho-Siberian core. The agradki were generally constructed in a row at a certain distance from the kurgans. The accompanying balbals lie eastwards of the memorial monuments. Finally, secondary graves related to far more recent periods were sometimes built on top of the Scytho-Siberian kurgans. Such is the main cluster pattern. The second group consists of various structures from different periods lying muddled up along both edges of the lower part of the valley. A third group consists of solitary structures scattered all over the valley.

PETROGLYPHS - The study of petroglyphs was the second part of archaeological research in the Sebÿstei valley. All petroglyphs were made by means of a simple pecking technique. They were mostly engraved on quartz veined metamorphic boulders. The depicted subjects were generally wild animals, with a dominance of little, isolated caprids. The distribution map shows that the engravings are not scattered all over the landscape. Even more, they are restricted to two specific areas, almost devoid of any archaeological structure. Although it is very difficult to

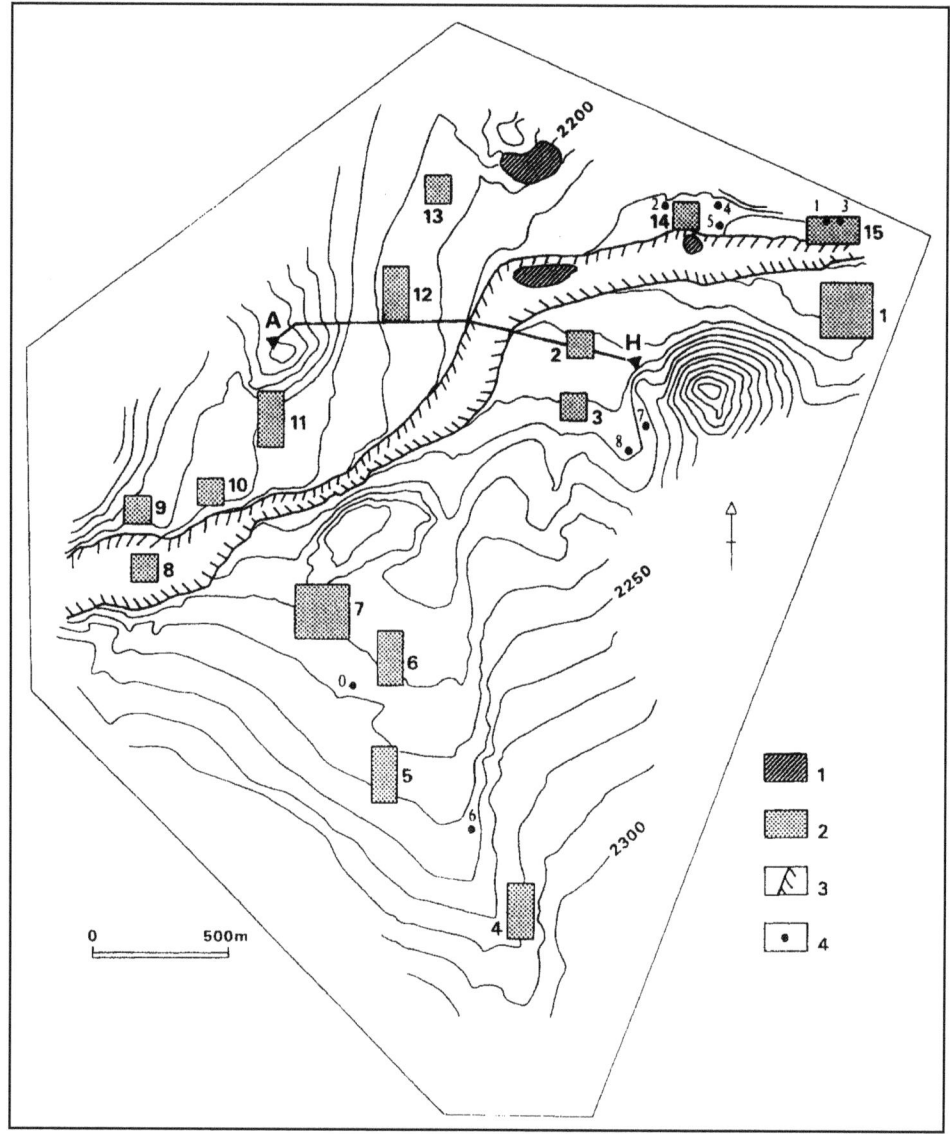

Figure 3. Sebystei: GPS-map of the central part of the valley (1: very active periglacial zones; 2: archaeological clusters (1-15); border of the actuel floodplain of the river; 4: localisation of rock samples; A-H: cross profile).

date, we have some reasons to assume that most of the petroglyphs date from the Scytho-Siberian period.

CONCLUSION - The survey of the archaeological structures and the petroglyphs shows that this small, closed valley had an active occupational history, at least during the Scytho-Siberian and the Turkic period. Despite a large number of monuments, no indications of ancient permanent or temporary settlements were discovered. All structures have a clear ritual or burial function. Taking into consideration the absence of settlements and the pedological data, which indicate that the environment has not really changed since the Scytho-Siberian period, it may be assumed that this valley was always a locus of activities related to the "spiritual world". The only economical activities that took place here were probably herding - as it is nowadays. The structures were erected in the three different geographical entities of the valley, with a clear preference for the middle part. In that area, monuments are mostly clustered and situated on the flat terraces. The clustering and the large uniformity of the petroglyphs also seems to be intentional. Therefore, it is suggested that archaeological structures and petroglyphs are part of one ritual landscape, in which the former are related to the centre, the latter to the edges of the valley.

KALANEGIR VALLEY (1997)

During the summer of 1997 similar research was carried out in the Kalanegir valley. The Kalanegir is an important tributary of the Tarkhata river. The latter is of old an important passage between the south-eastern Altai region and the Mongolian highlands, with the Chuya depression and the Ukok plateau as its nodes.

The lower part of the Kalanegir valley (2200 m.a.s.l. near its confluence with the Tarkhata) is characterised by lodgement and melt out till deposits (the data are published *in extensu* in Bourgeois e.a. 1999b). The results of the survey are to a large extend comparable to those of the Sebÿstei valley. Only the differences will shortly be mentioned.

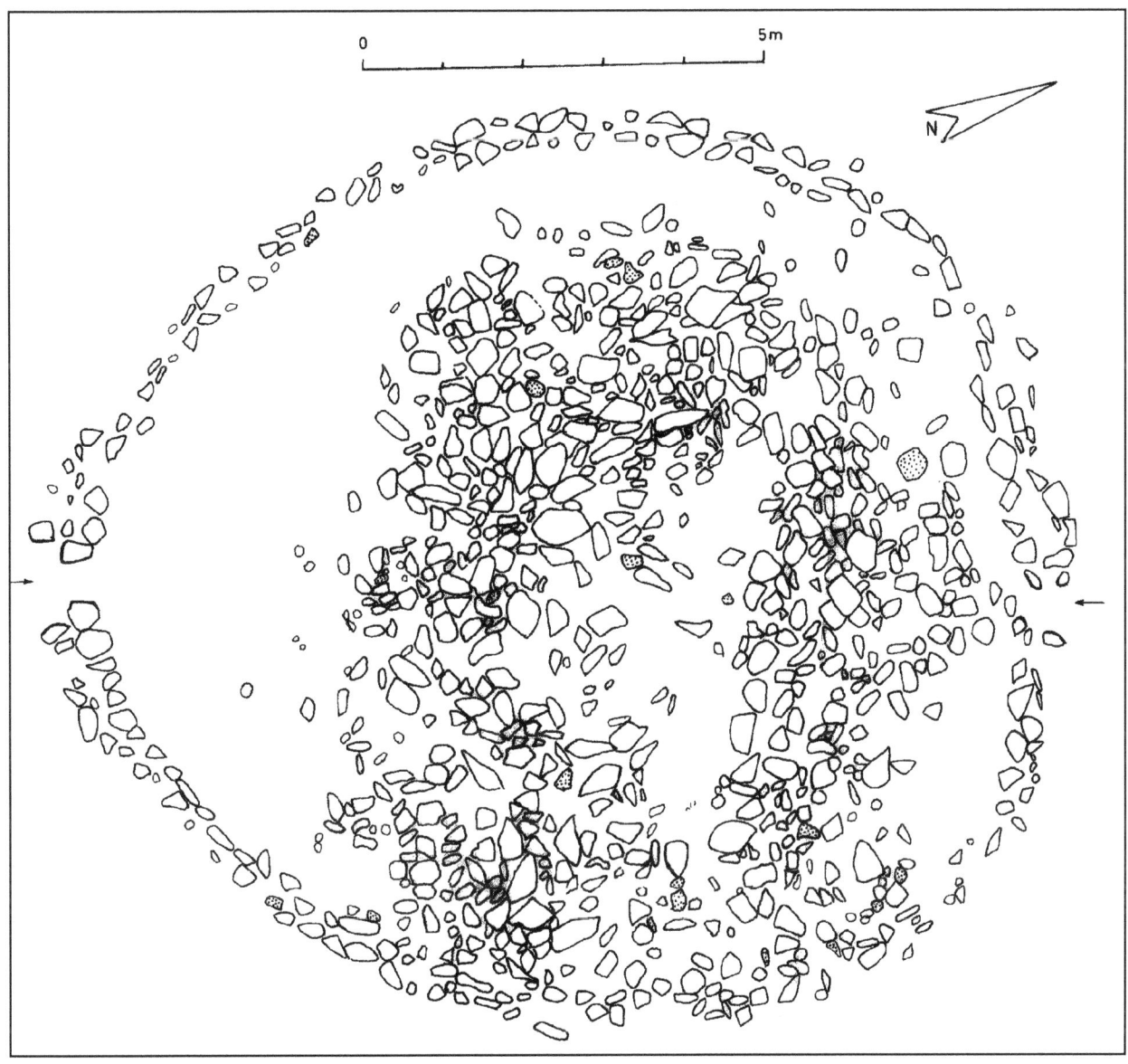

Figure 4. Sebystei: Bronze Age cairn, the outer circle has two opposite "entrances" (n° 25).

STRUCTURES - 56 archaeological structures were built in this valley (32 Scytho-Siberian kurgans, 2 contemporaneous ritual circles, 15 Turkic agradki and 7 unnatural concentrations of stones). One cluster (four in total) is situated in a permafrost area and was subjected to specific pedological and geophysical research (fig. 5). Several questions are raised by these 1 observations. Did the permafrost exist at the time of construction of the kurgans? Does the presence of natural permafrost imply the presence of a frozen burial chamber? To which extend did the natural permafrost preserve the organic material inherent to these burial structures? Only excavations can provide a clear answer to these relevant and important questions.

PETROGLYPHS – In Kalanegir two engravings representing bovids are dated to the Bronze Age. The petroglyphs are made at three locations, specific transitional zones in the valley or dominant features in the landscape.

CONCLUSION – The study of a permafrost zone with archaeological structures, mostly Scytho-Siberian kurgans, shows the value of basic pedological and geophysical surveys on archaeological sites to provide an insight into the natural conditions of the site and the surrounding environment. These techniques have the advantage that they are little or non-destructive, easy to execute, cheap and fast. They can be seen as an ideal instrument for the archaeological community to detect potential frozen tombs in the Altai Mountains and elsewhere. An increase in active layer thickness of 10 to 20 % is predicted for the middle of the next century (Anisimov e.a. 1997). These predictions are based on active layer thickness calculation using predicted climatic data generated by General Circulation Models. It is also expected that the occurrence of discontinuous permafrost in the Altai Mountains will significantly diminish. It is clear that all archaeological structures underlain by natural permafrost or containing anthropogenic ice lenses are vulnerable to these predicted climatic changes, and might disappear. Thus, the archaeological community cannot afford procrastination in determining its policy towards these scientific and culturally extremely valuable frozen witnesses of the past.

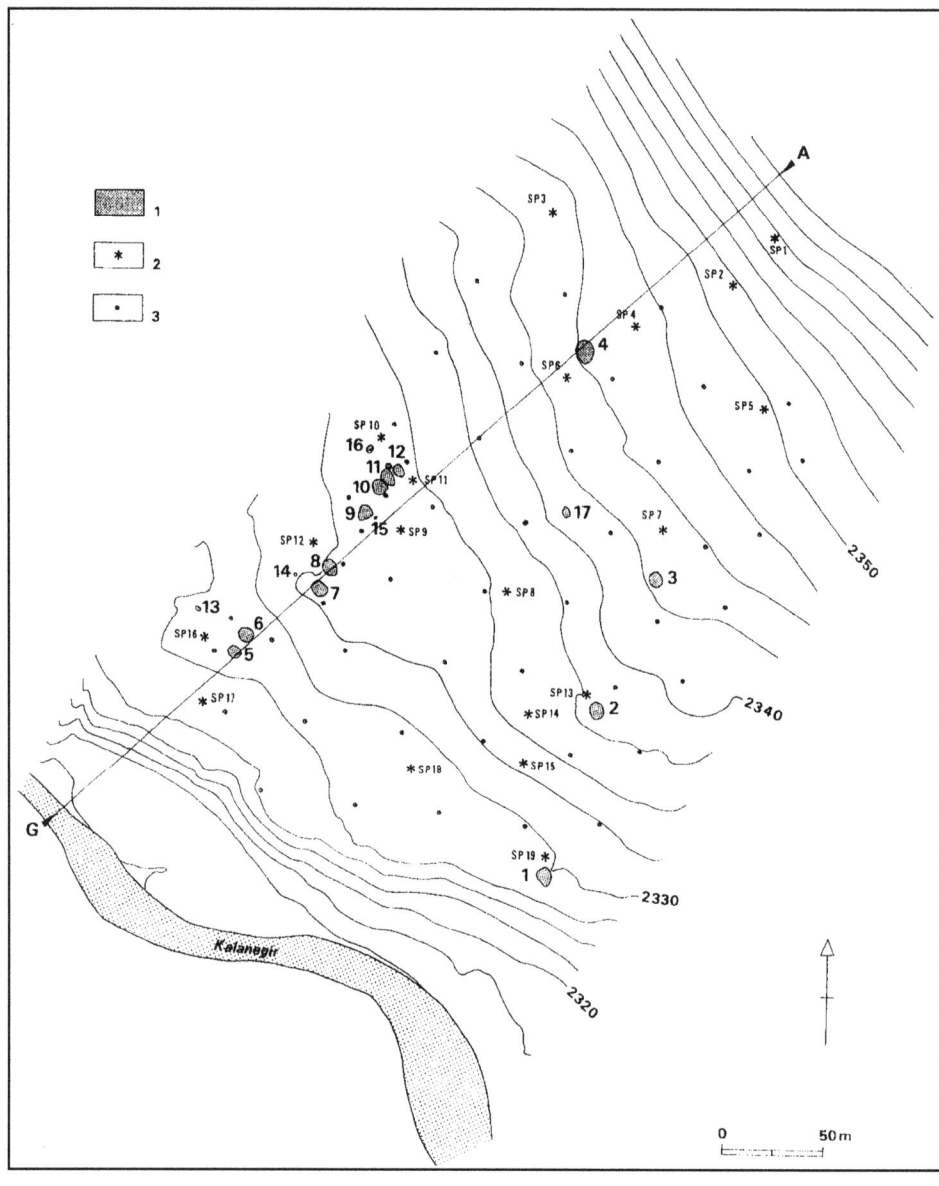

Figure 5. Kalanegir: topographical map of "the permafrost site"
(1: archaeological structures; 2: soil profiles; 3: auger observations).

UJMONSKI STEPPE (1999)

Having completed surveys during two summers in the high mountains area where human impact is negligible, it was decided to change the focus towards lower lying areas where human impact is clearer. In 1999 the left bank of the so-called Ujmonski steppe was the subject of some new research. The Ujmonski steppe is a large intramontaneous depression at an altitude of 1000 m.a.s.l. in the southwestern part of the Republic. The whole area, at least the flat middle part, is cultivated. One will find fields, meadows and pastures. So, it is not surprising to find the sites more or less exclusively on the slopes of the depression. The survey was done together with Sergei Kire'ev (Gorno-Altaisk State University) who surveyed the area already once in 1991. About 150 structures representing more than 50 sites were found. Most sites were exclusively made up of Scytho-Siberian kurgans (fig. 6). Smaller structures as balbals or agradki were not found at all. The same holds for petroglyphs.

The main conclusion that should be drawn after the 1999 research is triple:

– firstly, the archaeological monuments are damaged, and for the medium long period destroyed, by human activities (agriculture but also construction works). A marked difference with the situation in 1991 could be observed. Protection measures are necessary;

– secondly, it was not always easy to find back sites localised in 1991. The localisation of the archaeological heritage should be done in a meticulous way using modern precise techniques (GPS linked to a GIS);

– finally, the intense new survey brought to light a lot of unknown monuments, amongst them the best preserved of the region.

This research showed very clearly how important archaeological surveys are for a well established heritage management, especially in an agrarian area.

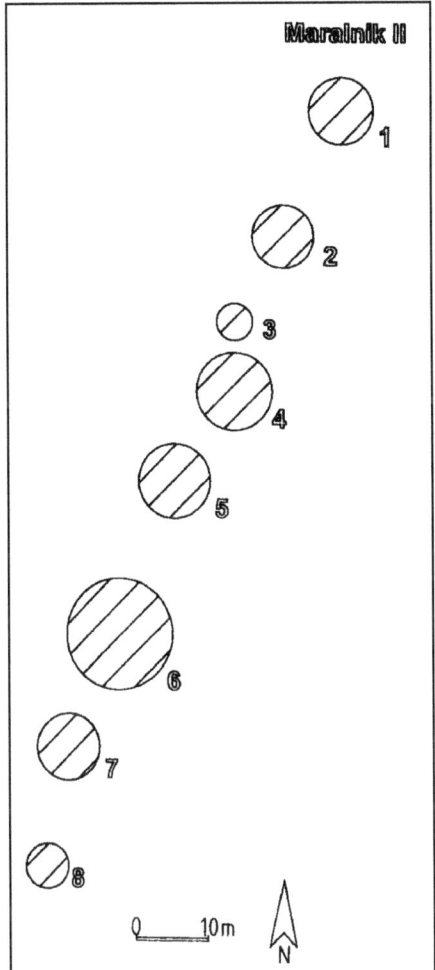

Figure 6. Ujmonski steppe: the site of Maralnik II: a typical alignment of eight north-south orientated Scytho-Siberian kurgans.

MAIMA (2000)

The campaign in 2000 focused on the study of the Maima area. Maima is situated along the right bank of the Katun' river to the North of Gorno-Altaisk, the capital of the Republic. This area had also already been surveyed by Sergei Kire'ev.

The main objective of this campaign was a small excavation on a Scytho-Siberian settlement in order to explore the possible relationship with contemporaneous kurgans situated in the immediate vicinity. Unfortunately, no archaeological structures were recognised. Neverthe-less, a huge amount of early Scytho-Siberian pottery and some stone and metal artifacts were found in the covering chernozem horizon. At a deeper level, the remnants of a mesolithic site were found *in situ*.

Adjoining this excavation, the opportunity was seized to locate precisely - using a GPS - the different sites in the area. This research still needs to be finalised, but it seems as if a pattern in the occupation of the area can be recognised. Each part of the first river terrace (i.e. geographical units separated by small tributaries of the Katun') seems to hold a large Scytho-Siberian settlement and a Scytho-Siberian graveyard. On the other terraces, mostly smaller, settlements were found. Additional research should be done in order to verify whether these observations are true or not.

CONCLUSION

After half a decade of research in the Altai Republic, we hope to have shown that further research focused on surveys and inventories is of primary importance for the cultural heritage of the Republic. In this perspective, our Department is investigating if the use of satellite images (CORONA pictures of the CIA) can be useful in the detection and interpretation of archaeological structures. The first results are promising.

Authors' Address

Ignace BOURGEOIS
Jean BOURGEOIS
Ghent University
Department of Archaeology and Ancient History of Europe
Blandijnberg 2
B-9000 Gent BELGIUM
Email : Ignace.Bourgeois@rug.ac.be
Email : Jean.Bourgeois@rug.ac.be
http://www.flwi.rug.ac.be/AAHE/altaien-intro.htm

Bibliography

ANISIMOV, O.A., SHIKLOMANOV, N.I. & NELSON, F.E., 1997, Global warming and active-layer thickness: results from transient general circulation models. *Global and Planetary Change* 15, p. 61-77.

BOURGEOIS, I., BOURGEOIS, J., CAMMAERT, L., DECLEIR, H., LANGOHR, R., MIKKELSEN, J.H. & VAN HUELE, W., 1999a, Multidisciplinary archaeological research in the Sebÿstei valley 1996-1997 (Kosh-Agash region, Altai Republic). *Eurasia Antiqua* 5, p. 295-389.

BOURGEOIS, I., MIKKELSEN, J.H., VAN HOOF, L., VAN HUELE, W., BOURGEOIS, J., LANGOHR, R., CAMMAERT, L. & DECLEIR, H., 1999b, An archaeological survey of the Kalanegir valley (Kosh-Agach region, Altai Republic): petroglyphs and Scytho-Siberian kurgans in a discontinuous permafrost area. A multidisciplinary approach. *Ancient civilizations from Scythia to Siberia* 6 (1-2), p. 77-101.

BOURGEOIS, I., CAMMAERT, L., MASSART, C., MIKKELSEN, J.H. & VAN HUELE, W., 2000, *Ancient nomads of the Altai Mountains. Belgian-Russian multidiscip-inary archaeological research on the Scytho-Siberian culture*. Brussels: Royal Museums of Art and History.

CAHEN-DELHAYE, A. (red.), 1991, *L'or des Scythes*. Brussels: Royal Museums of Art and History.

CHANG, C., TOURTELOTTE, P.A., BAIPAKOV, K.M. & GREGORIEV, F.P., 1999, The Kazakh-American Talgar project archaeological field surveys in 1997 and 1998 in the Talgar region. *Chabarlari Izvestia* 1 (219), p. 168-185.

DEREVIANKO, A.P., MOLODIN, V.I. (ed.), 2000, *Phenomenon of the Altai mummies*. Novosibirsk: Institute of Archaeology and Ethnography Press (in Russian).

JACOBSON, E. & MEACHAM, J.E., 1998, When stones speak: mapping and Mongolian surface archaeology. *Geo Info Systems* 8 (2), p. 14-22.

KUBAREV, V.D., 1991, *The kurgans of the Yustyd valley*. Novosibirsk: "Nayka" Sibirskoe Otdelenie (in Russian).

KUBAREV, V.D., 1992, *The kurgans of the Sailyugem valley*. Novosibirsk: "Nayka" Sibirskoe Otdelenie (in Russian).

RUDENKO, S.I., 1970, *Frozen tombs of Siberia. The Pazyryk burials of Iron Age horsemen*. London: J.M. Dent & Sons Ltd.

SAMASHEV, Z.S., BAZARBAEVA, G.A., ZHUMABEKOVA, G.S. & FRANCFORT, H.-P., 2000, Le kourgane de Berel' dans l'Altaï kazakhstanais, *Arts Asiatiques* 55, p. 5-20.

ANCIENT HUNTER-GATHERERS, FIRST SEDENTARY FARMERS AND NOMAD STOCK HERDERS OF MONGOLIA (8000-3000 BC): NEW RESEARCHES AT TAMSAGBULAG (DORNOD AIMAK)

Michel Louis SEFERIADES

Résumé : Cette communication fait état des premiers résultats de la Mission Archéologique Française en Mongolie pour la Période Néolithique. Il est question ici, dans le cadre des recherches récentes sur les aspects originaux des processus de néolithisation eurasiatiques et les techniques modernes de l'archéologie dans le domaine de la protohistoire (Mésolithique/Néolithique, début de l'Holocène), des prospections et fouilles dans la région de Tamsagbulag (Mongolie orientale, département (aimak) du Dornod) anciennement étudiée par une mission soviéto-mongole dirigée par le célèbre archéologue russe A.P. Okladnikov.

Abstract: The article outlines the first results of the French Archaeological Mission to Mongolia centered on Neolithic. The topics discussed include the general aspects of the initial Neolithisation in Eurasia, and the use of state-of-the art archaeological techniques in the studies on Prehistory, with special reference to Mesolithic/Neolithic interface, as exemplified by the survey and excavations in the area of Tamsagbulag site (Eastern Mongolia, aimak/ditrct/ of Dornod) originally investigated by a Soviet-Mongolian mission directed by Professor A.P. Okladnikov, a renowned Russian archaelogist.

I would like to discuss here, the project of the *French Archaeological Mission in Mongolia for the Neolithic Period*. This project covers Outer Mongolia, half way between Russia (Siberia) to the North, Kazakhstan to the West and China (Inner Mongolia and Manchuria), Korea and Japan to the South and East.

Despite the fact that more than a thousand Palaeolithic sites are recorded and that period is relatively well known there, this was not the case of the Neolithic (*a fortiori* for the Mesolithic). In the words of my colleague and friend Professor Jacques Legrand (INALCO, Paris), "Research into the Neolithic of Mongolia should provide information and essential hypotheses which would improve our knowledge of the rise and formation of Central Asiatic nomadic pastoralism (particularly Mongolian), a phenomenon which dominated the historic period throughout the central and eastern part of Eurasia." At the beginning and concurrently with the North-Pontic and Danubian areas, waves of nomadic pastoralists (Proto-Indo-Europeans in the opinion of many of my colleagues) disrupted the established economic and social structures of the sedentary Neolithic and Eneolithic groups (the Cucuteni-Tripolye, Gumelnitsa, Karanovo VI, etc.) introducing, among other novelties, the horse and wheel.

Amazingly, more is known of dinosaurs' fossil eggs and bones in the Gobi Desert than of the Neolithic in Mongolia! But, despite the paucity of publications, there is a fair amount of actual data available. At the Department of Archaeology of the Institute of History at Ulaan Baatar, with the help of my Mongolian colleague B. Gunchinsuren, I started a personal inventory of Mesolithic and Neolithic sites, putting them on the map. I also started to study the stone tools and ceramic assemblages, primarily based on unpublished and poorly known Soviet and Mongolian surveys and excavations.

Based on that, I identified four regions of Mesolithic and Neolithic socio-economic and cultural entities:

1 - Region West of the Altai and West of the Khangai Mountains.

2 - North-Central region South of Lake Baikal.

3 - Southern region in the North of China (the Northern Gobi).

4 - Eastern region in the North and West of Manchuria.

Yet this pattern results rather from the state of our knowledge than a carefully designed research strategy. It is mainly based on surface finds (stone tools, sherds, etc.). Results of systematic excavations are few, especially in chronostratigraphic sequences. The only excavation worthy of its name is that of the Soviet Mission directed (first in 1949 and then 1967) by the renowned Russian archaeologist A.P. Okladnikov at the Mesolithic/Neolithic site of Tamsagbulag (Eastern Mongolia, Dornod aimak).

THE FRENCH ARCHAEOLOGICAL MISSION IN MONGOLIA FOR THE NEOLITHIC PERIOD

The *French Archaeological Mission in Mongolia for the Neolithic Period* was established in 1996 under the auspices of French Foreign Office and the Mongolian Academy of Sciences (Institute of History), with the intention, as its first objective, of undertaking remote sensing, excavations and surveys at Tamsagbulag. Despite the briefness of the reports on earlier Soviet excavations (essentially by A.P. Okladnikov & A.P. Derevianko, 1970, D. Dorj, 1971), it became clear that this was a key Mesolithic/Neolithic site in Central Asia, and this was confirmed by both the materials of these excavations and by two recent syntheses by A.P. Derevianko & D. Dorj (1992) and A.P. Derevianko (1994).

Tamsagbulag is the key site for the Tamsagbulag Culture, which, in my opinion (see below), dates to the 5th millennium BC. The occupants were both sedentary hunter-fisher-gatherers and farmers. Semi-subterranean dwellings

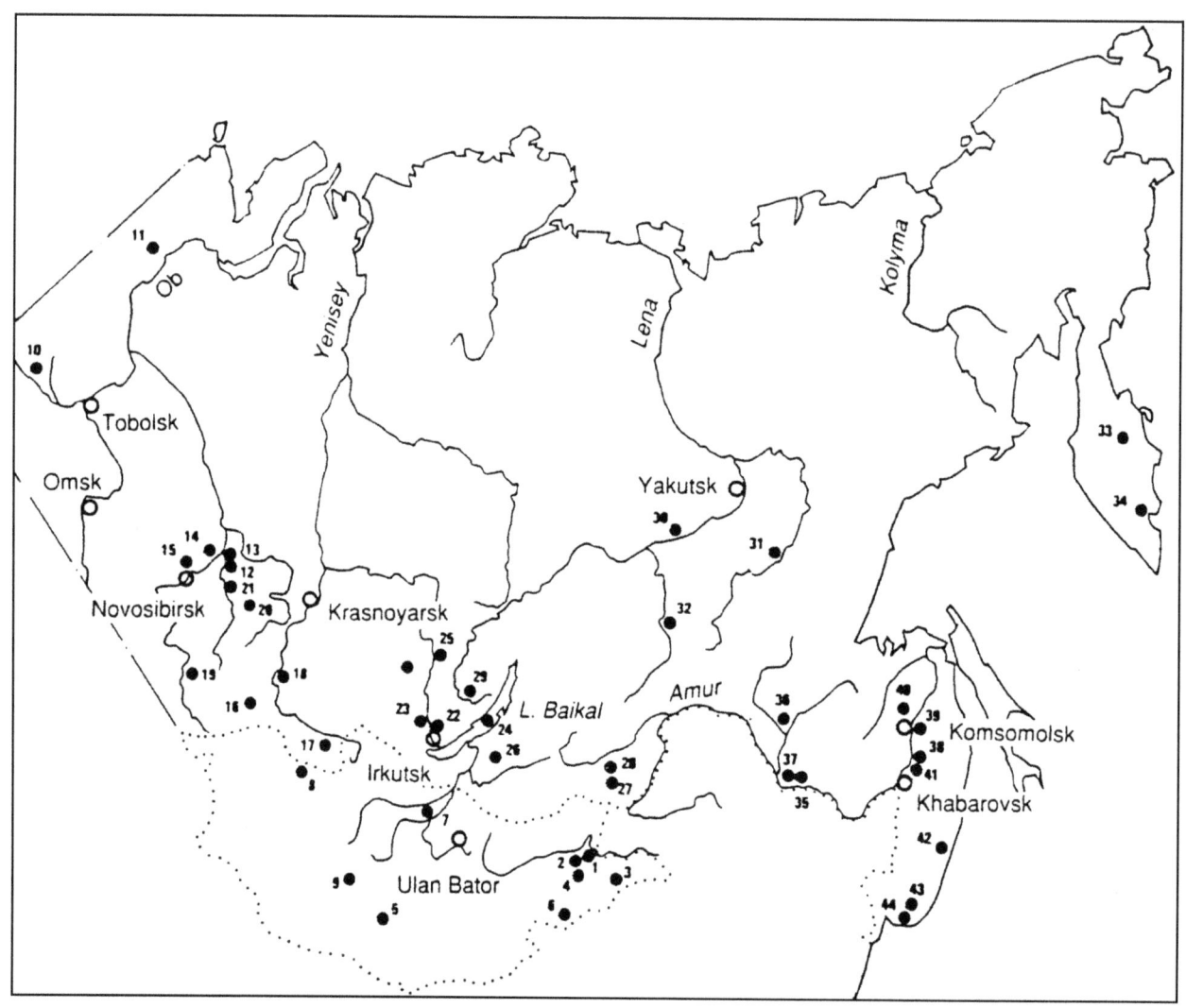

Figure 1. Most important Neolithic sites in central and northern Asia (after A.P. Derevianko 1994):
1. Yamat Nuur, 2. Ovoot, 3. Tamsagbulag, 4. Khuitynbulag, 5. Shabarak, 6. Daringanga, 7. Arshan-Khad, 8. Chandman, 9. Uldzit, 10. Andreyevskoe lake, 11. Ches-tyi-yaga, 12. the Samus burials, 13. the Tomsk burials, 14. Alexandrovskoe, 15.Zavjalovo, 16. Ust-Khemchik, 17. Toorakhem, 18. Khadynnykh, 19. Kuyum, 20. the Vaskovskoe burial, 21. the Tomsk petroglyphs, 22. Lenkovka, 23. the Chastaya and Khinskaya valleys, 24. Olkhon, 25. Kamennye isles, 26. Mukhinskoe, 27. Chindant, 28. Budulan, 29. Shishkino, 30. Kullaty, 31. Belkachi, 32. Krestyakh, 33. Ushkovskaya, 34. Tarya, 35. Novopetrovka, 36. Gromatukha, 37. Osinovoe lake, 38. Malyshevo, 39. Voznesenska, 40. Kondon, 41. Sakachi-Alyan, 42. Rudnaya, 43. Zaisanovska, 44. Kirovskoe.

(with posts supporting the roof) oriented South-East to North-West (around 40 m^2: 7.60 m long, 5.60 m large and 0.60 m under the soil) with storage pits and burials inside the houses have been found. Stone (chipped and polished) and bone tool assemblages, ceramic materials are rich as are paleobotanical and faunal samples (millet, large fish, bird, cattle, pig, horse, etc.). A bull cult (?) inherited from the Palaeolithic times (see Séfériadès M. & Stanko V. (2000): bisons of Anetovka in Ukraine) has been identified (a pit filled with the bones of that animal).

THE 1997 FIELD SEASON'

Tamsagbulag ("bulag" meaning "spring" in Mongolian) lies South-East of the town of Choibalsan, in the desert-steppe region just a few kilometres off the Chinese border (Manchuria), a region that was abundant in black-tailed gazelles and saiga antelopes before (that is what people are saying) the Soviet Army finished them off... It forms part of a large lake which today is almost completely dry, one-two kilometres wide between the higher southern terraces (Tamsagbulag 1) and the lower northern ones (Tamsagbulag 2). In the North, we were able to locate the remains of the village of Tamsagbulag built of mud-bricks and abandoned some fifty years ago (?). A few kilometres to the North-East one may note series of small lakes located South of a larger lake, the Buir.

Tamsagbulag 1

With some difficulty we were able to locate the site of Tamsagbulag 1 identified on the basis of its position in relation to a cliff ten-twelve metres high and with a spring at its foot, mentioned in a brief publication of A.P. Okladnikov and A.P. Derevianko.

It seems possible that Mesolithic and Neolithic hunters of gazelle and antelope were based here in much the same way as Magdalenian hunters awaited the reindeer on the

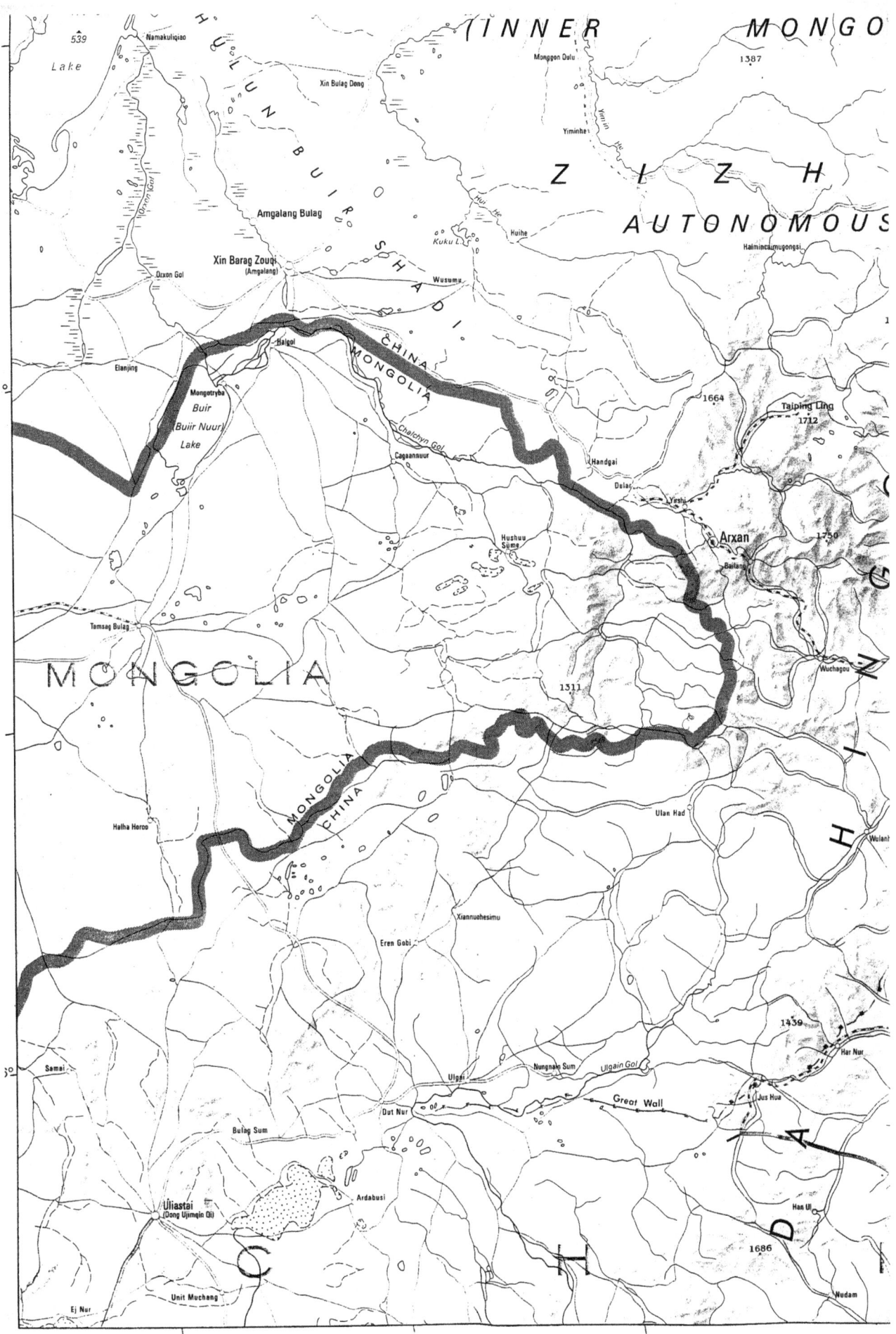

Figure 2. Location of Tamsagbulag (Dornod aimak/district of Eastern Mongolia).

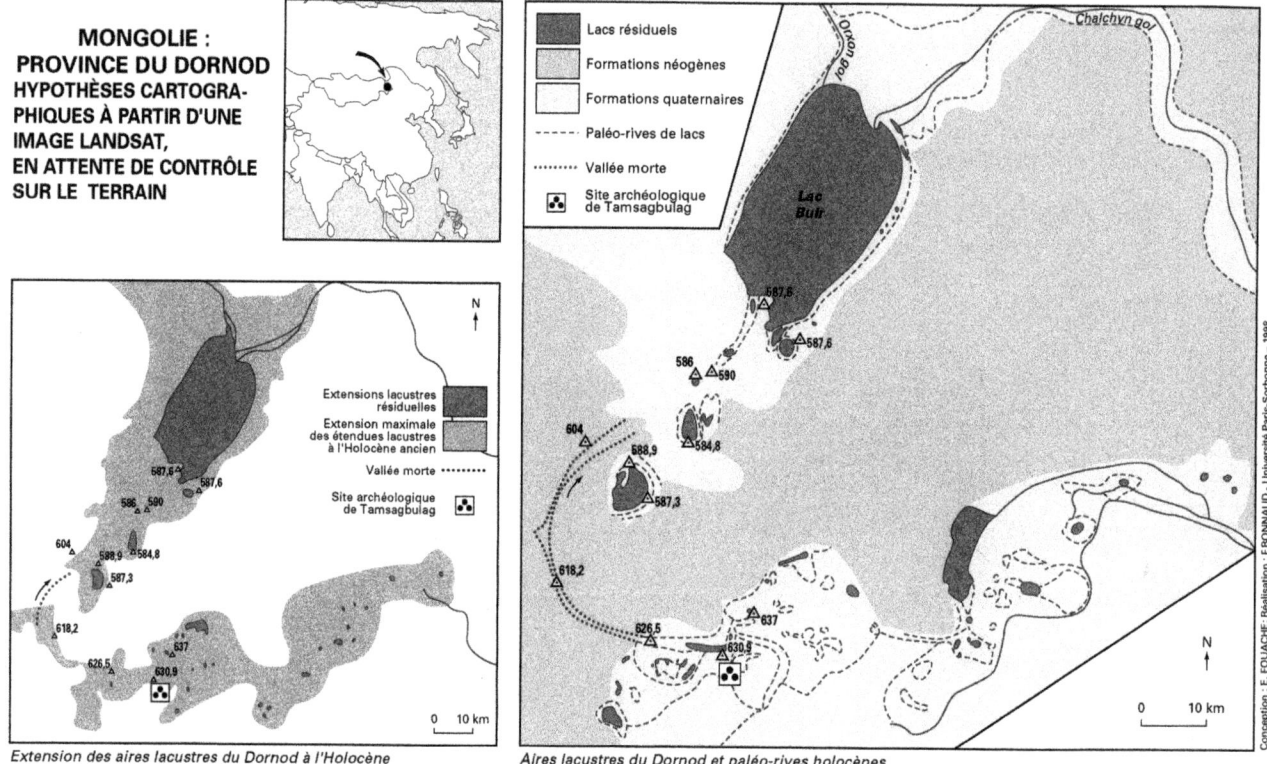

Figure 3. Tamsagbulag: Analysis of satellite imagery (Landsat TM) by E. Fouache (University of Paris-Sorbonne 1998) showing a clear system of palaeo-shore-lines indicative of a regression of the lake during the Holocene.

Figure 4. Tamsgbulag 1: Trench A seen from the South. Spring ("bulag" in Mongolian) at the foot of the terrace (12m high); the marshy area and the soviet built milatary road through the ancient lake; on the background, the opposite terraces (Tamsagbulag 2) and the steppe.

left bank of the Seine at Pincevent and during the Late Upper Paleolithic, on the Bug terrace in the Ukraine, bison herds were taken at Anetovka more than ten thousand years ago (Séfériadès & Stanko 2000).

Figure 5. Tamsagbulag 3: The Mésolithic/Neolithic site (palaeo-shorelines) discovered in 1997 during the first mission.

Figure 6. Tamsagbulag 3: Fragments of pottery found associated with a microlithic industry on the sand-dunes of the palaeo-shore-lines.

During the first campaign (August/September 1997), two complementary strategies were adopted:

1 - Intensive surveys yielded several hundred stone tools, including several polished ones, and a significant number of potsherds suggesting affinity with the Neolithic of the Lake Baikal and Amur region of Siberia and contemporary groups in South-East Asia.

2 - Four trenches (A, B, C and D) from 1 to 4 m² in size were dug:

- Trench A, 4 m² on the higher terrace, a few metres away from the cliff facing the spring, while yielding no archaeological material has provided an excellent stratigraphy for sedimentological and palynological analyses. Two stratigraphic exposures to the East-

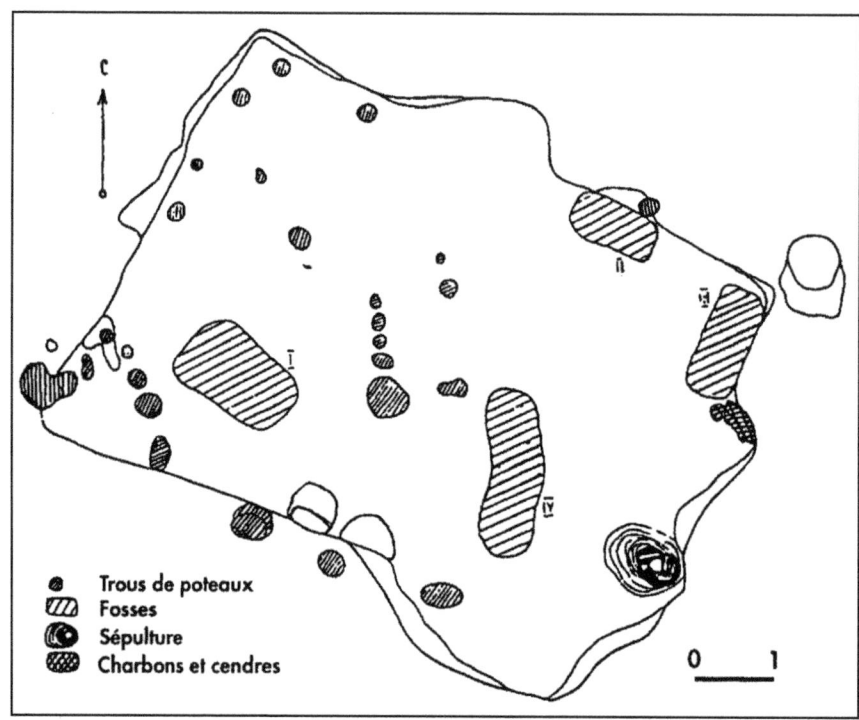

Figure 7. Tamsagbulag 1: Plan of a semi-subterranean house (after A.P. Okladnikov & A.P. Derevianko, 1970).

Figure 8. Village of Kamchatka with a winter semi-subterranean house.
Note: The only way of access is via aperture in the roof (after Cook, 1785).

West and North-South provided a sequence for the upper terrace occupied during the Neolithic: below the vegetal topsoil (20cm) there was a sequence of sand (90cm) underlain by the compact clayey soil.

The latter caused us to stop the excavations. The stratigraphy provided information on the formation of the upper terrace, the palaeoclimate, the landscape, biotopes and ecosystems of the semi-

Figure 9. Inside look of a house from Alaska. The only way of access, using a trunk with incised steps, is also via an aperture in the roof (after Cook, 1785).

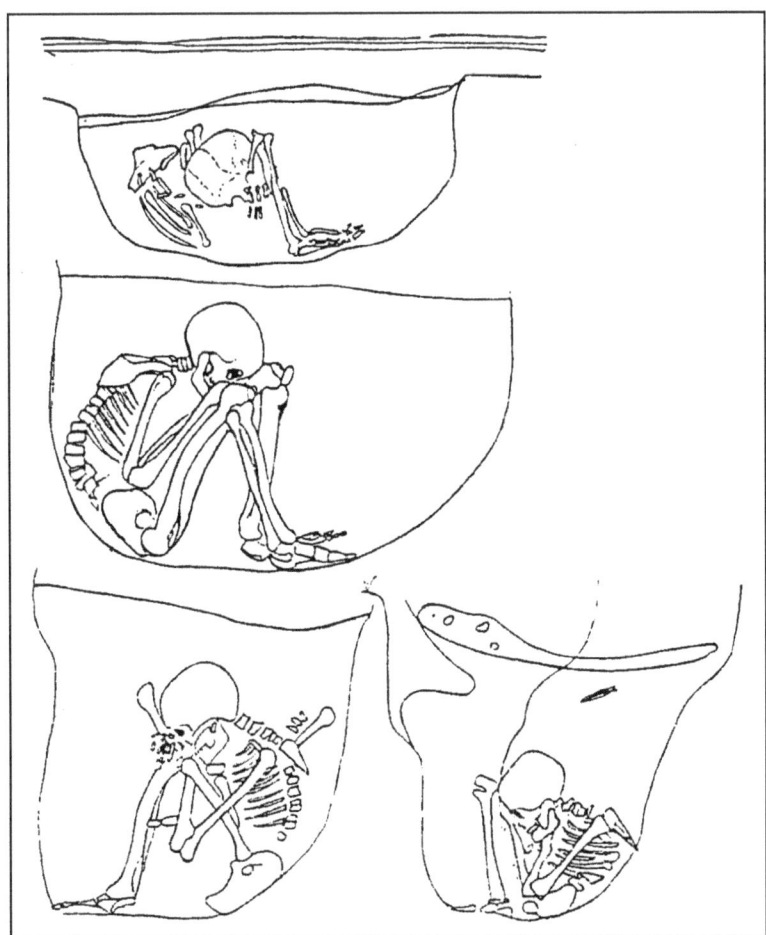

Figure 10. Tamsagbulag 1: Types of graves discovered beneath the soil of the houses (after A.P. Okladnikov & A.P. Derevianko, 1970).

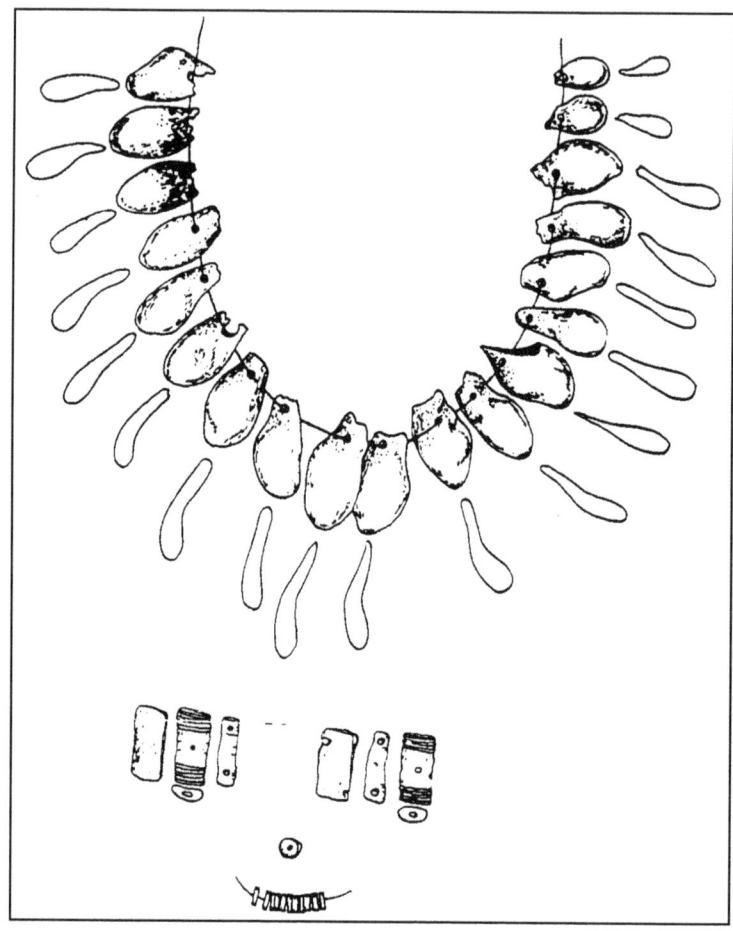

Figure 11. Tamsagbulag 1: Necklace of stag canines, plate and tubular beads of pearl (*Unio*) from the graves (after A.P. Okladnikov & A.P. Derevianko, 1970).

Figure 12. Tamsagbulag 1: Polished pestle fragment.

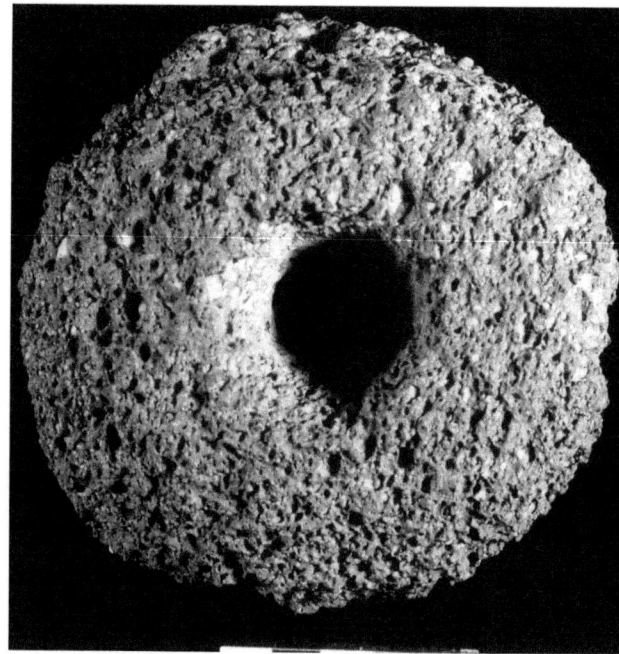

Figure 13. Tamsagbulag 3: Perforated circular tool (for digging sticks?) in volcanic rock.

Figure 14. Tamsagbulag 1: Incised and channeled grey ware.

Figure 15. Tamsagbulag 1: Corded ware.

sedentary Mesolithic/Neolithic groups, at the beginning of the Holocene.

- Trenches B and C, two hundred metres South of the spring. Only trench B yielded chipped stone artefacts (Neolithic).

- Trench D (3 m²) at the foot of the terrace, not far from the spring, yielded the upper part of the brown and yellow Neolithic layer mixed with charcoal and ash (with chipped stone tools, fragments of pottery). A C^{14} date from this trench (Gif.10949) of 5590 ± 120 has been obtained (calibrated: 4753/4155 BC). This date is of the same order as the dates for Neolithic sites obtained in China.

Figure 16. Tamsagbulag 1: Fragments of discs allegedly used for cooking cereal pancakes or bread.

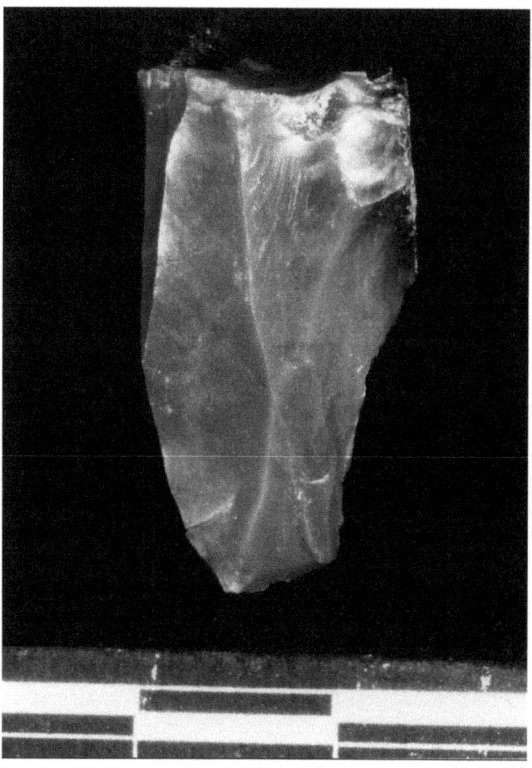

Figure 17. Tamsagbulag 1: Microlithic industry: Nucleus.

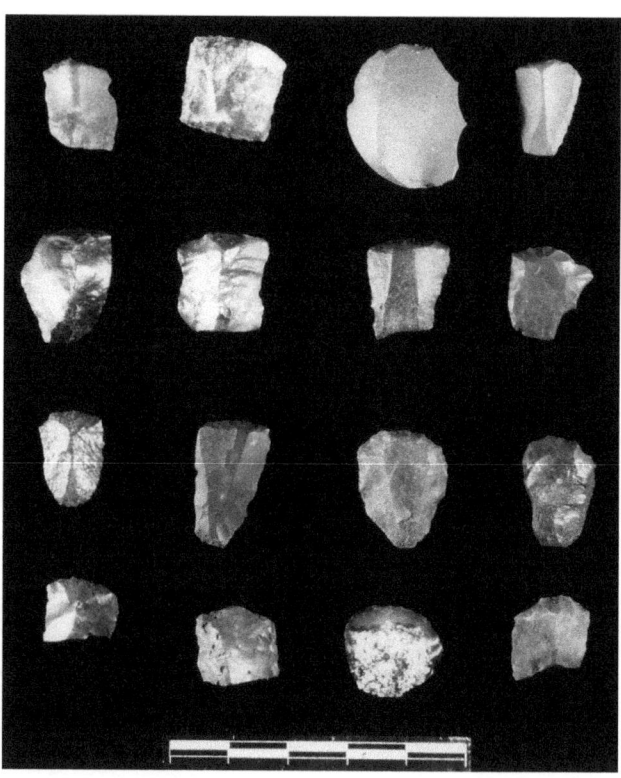

Figure 18. Tamsagbulag 1: Microlithic industry: scrapers.

Tamsagbulag 2

Tamsagbulag 2 is a new site discovered on the opposite (northern) bank of the ancient lake. There, over a hundred metres on both sides of the remains of the "Soviet Army bridge", a brief investigation yielded chipped stone artefacts and ceramic assemblages which belong predominantly to historic times. A few metres to the West of the military bridge, remains of a Tibetan monastery (?), a temple and a sort of clay hearth with numerous vases and other cultual objects were found.

Figure 19. Tamsagbulag 1: Microlithic industry: bladelets and scrapers.

Figure 20. Tamsagbulag 1: Chipped stone industry: Tamsagbulag-type scrapers (small plaquettes with abruptly retouched edges).

Tamsagbulag 3

Tamsagbulag is yet another new site, discovered on the eastern side of the ancient lake; it lies to the North-North-East of Tamsagbulag 1. A small lake, almost completely dried up today, is surrounded by small sand dunes. Intensive reconnaissance on the eastern bank of the lake, below the small terrace and on the gentle (windward) slope of the dune, has yielded important lithic and ceramic materials. Artefacts collected came from a Neolithic camp or habita-

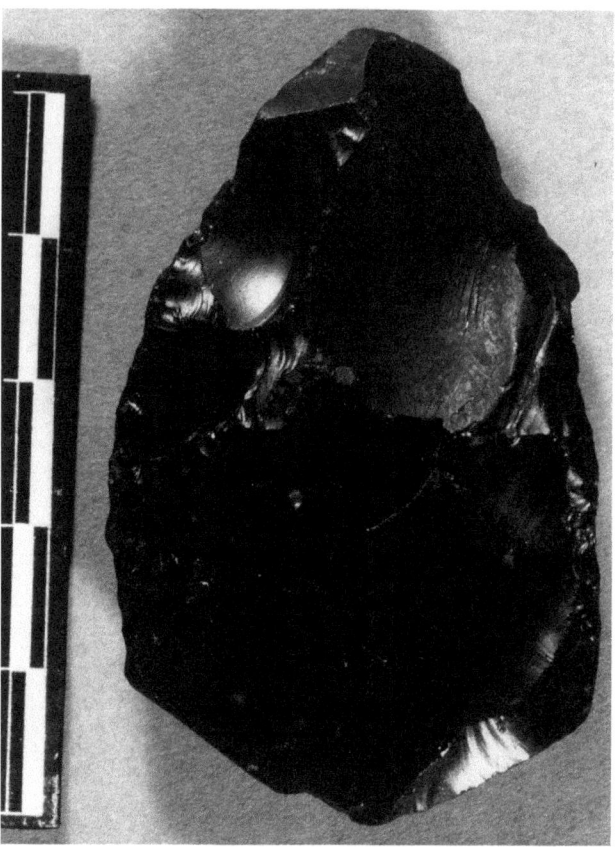

Figure 21. Tamsagbulag 1: Unifacially flaked leaf point in black rock (phtanite)

Figure 23. Tamsagbulag 1: Chipped stone industry: Obsidian fragments.

tion site, located not far from the terrace. Chipped stone industry and sherds were concentrated at the foot of the terrace.

In the areas of a dense concentration of lithics and pottery, a long bone of gazelle or antelope (which appeared to be fossilised given the state of preservation) was recovered. The C^{14} date obtained (Gyf. 10945) places the site in the third millennium BC - more recent that of Tamsagbulag 1. Presumably, groups of Mesolithic hunters who became more sedentary in the process of Neolithisation, moved from the large dried out lake area of Tamsgbulag 1 of the fifth millennium, to the residual lake of Tamsagbulag 3 in the third millennium, prior to having to opt once again for a nomadic way of life - this time definitively.

ARCHAEOLOGICAL MATERIAL

Chipped stone industry

Several hundred pieces recovered suggest the occurrence of a rich assemblage. Raw material consists of local flint (opaque and translucent) and semi-precious stones of various colours (chalcedony, quartz, crystal, jasper, etc.). The microlithic industry dominates the secondary-chipped lithics. Small lake pebbles are notable and are being analysed. One should note: prismatic nuclei, pyramidal nuclei, subpyramidal nuclei, bladelet nuclei (the "Gobi"-type cores), the products of pressure flaking, standardised production using homogeneous raw material, morphologically varied blades and bladelets (as, for example, sickle microblades inserted into knives), blade scrapers, thick endscrapers, carinated scrapers, thumbnail (micro)scrapers

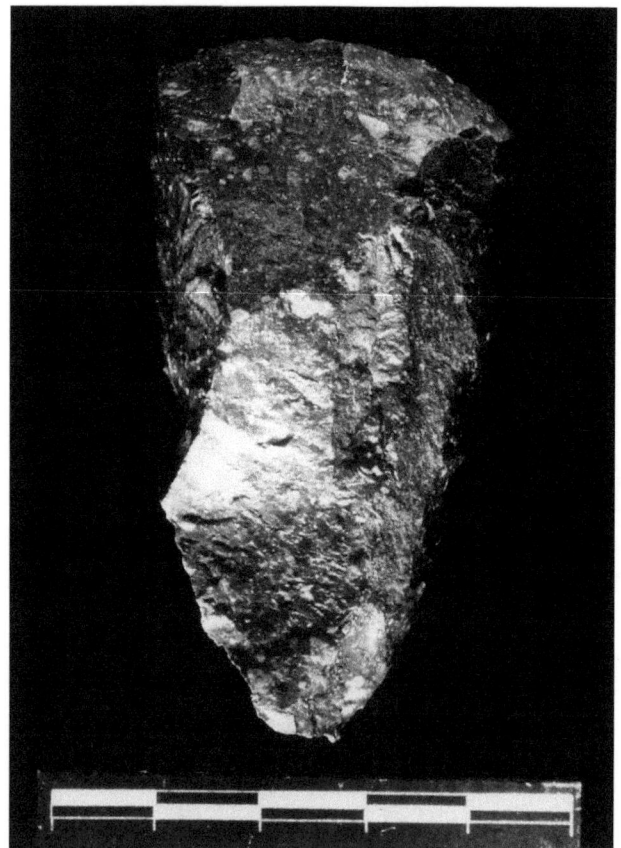

Figure 22. Tamsagbulag 1: Thick elongated end-scraper (in the Late Palaeolithic tradition).

Figure 24. Tamsagbulag 1: Chipped stone industry: Arrow-heads.

and Tamsagbulag scrapers, first recognised by A.P. Okladnikov (small plaquettes or fragments thereof of different shapes. Their edges are abruptly retouched). Burins and piercers are also present. A unifacially flaked leaf point in black stone (phtanite) comes from Tamsagbulag 1. Also a white quartz arrow head. True microliths (geometric) seem absent.

Polished stone industry

Only five pieces have been recovered: an axe or adze fragment; a pestle fragment; fragments of a large disc; a heavy perforated circular tool (for digging sticks?) in volcanic rock from Tamsagbulag 3, like the "brise-mottes" of the Andes. A.P. Okladnikov's excavations yielded a similar piece and millstones also in volcanic rock.

Bone industry

No bone tools have been found among the surface collection, but knives, dagger knives or sickles (stone bladelets mounted in a bone haft) are well represented in A.P. Okladnikov's excavation assemblages as items of jewellery (beads).

Ceramics

Surveys and excavations at Tamsagbulag 1, 2 and 3 have yielded fragments of Neolithic and early (?) Bronze Age pottery. Neolithic/EBA sherds are distinguished by its friable raw material with a high content of sand (and shell?) and grey surface, incised or impressed surfaces (also corded ware) with elementary geometrical motifs, some of which look like the pottery from South Siberia, the Amur valley, North-West China, Inner Mongolia and Manchuria, Korea and South- Eastern Asia. Discs were probably used for cereal pancakes or bread cooking.

Metallurgy

Metallurgy (bronze and iron) is only represented by objects and fragments dating from the Iron Age to the modern period.

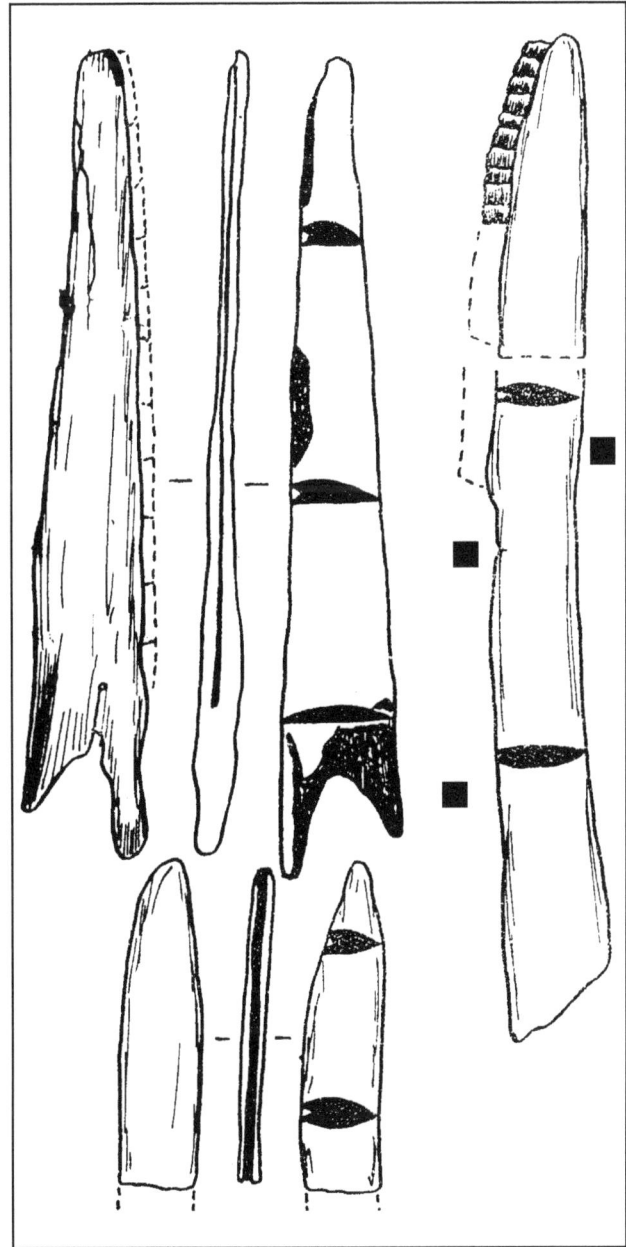

Figure 25. Bone industry (after D. Dorj, 1974).

Long distance exchange

Two pieces of obsidian, the millstone and the "brise-mottes" of volcanic tuffaceous rock, also fragments of jade (?) and several sherds of decorated pottery indicate the occurrence of medium-and long-distance exchange network patterns. One should also note a pendant (exhibited in the Museum of Ulaan Baatar) from one of the burials excavated by A.P. Okladnikov (?), presumably lapis lazuli of Afghanistan origin.

TAMSAGBULAG DEATH

Burials were found by A.P. Okladnikov under house floors with a series of grave goods (bone knives with inserted stone bladelets, necklaces of maral incisives and bone or mother of pearl beads (*Unio*), etc.). Remarkably, the skeletons were found in sitting position! Strange similarities with the mummies of the Ancient Peru (Chachapoyas, Chancay, Paracas, etc.) come to mind. Flexed and sitting position are unknown anywhere, and, especially in Europe, West, Central and South-East Asia. They may suggest an emigration through the Bering Strait from the primary Eurasian area (Mongolia and North-Eastern Siberia) to the Americas (Alaska and North America East coast) and then South to Central and South Americas.

FIRST CONCLUSIONS

The study of the site and its surrounding is indicative of a particular eco-system. Our field observations were corroborated by the analysis of satellite imagery (Landsat TM). E. Fouache, geomorphologist, points out (1998) that the terrain consists of a huge plateau at an altitude of 700 m, with two large depressions, one in the North, with the lake of Buir, and another in the south, with a string of small lakes. The Neogene sediments form the basement of the plateau, the Quaternary deposits filling in the depressions. Satellite imagery shows that the present-day lakes were interconnected (certainly at the beginning of the Holocene) by what is today a dry valley. Landsat images show clearly at Tamsagbulag a system of palaeo-shore-lines indicative of a regression of the lake, the depth of which never exceeded 12 m. An intensive evaporation in an environment of a dry steppe was the likely cause of this regression. This site is highly appropriate for the study of the Holocene climate fluctuations and its effects on the relief and human settlement.

The extension of the palaeo-lakes forms a key element in the prospecting of Neolithic sites in this area of the Dornod district (aimak) of Mongolia. Photos taken during our first mission in 1997 clearly show that sites were closely associated with the past hydrological network. Their exact topographic location is thus essential. In the absence of a strict topographic control, the map shown here is but a first approximation of the extent of rivers and lakes in the past.

It looks like as if the Mesolithic-Neolithic inhabitants of Tamsagbulag and neighbouring sites existed in an environment favouring partially predatory-type subsistence (hunting, fishing and food-gathering), their biotope being equally proper for food-producing (domestication of plants and animals). The process of Neolithisation was well under way, highlighting a new type of sedentism which accompanied the initial farming subsistence in this part of eastern central Mongolia.

The presently monotonous steppe-desert looked quite different during the three millennia that started 7,000 years ago. The climate then was mild and humid, vast grassland was abundant in marmots (*tarbagan* in Mongol), wolfs and eagles; stags and boars thrived in forests; small plots were located close to villages. Tamsagbulag consisted of several well separated houses located on the border of the elevated terrace, near the spring and stretching over the distance of 2-3 km. Looking from there, its inhabitants observed the herds of wild animals roving around the lake: black-tailed gazelle (*xarsuult zeer*), antelope saiga (*boxon*) and kulan (*xulan*). Hunters and fishers were direct heirs of their Mesolithic predecessors (arrows or spears with chipped stone or bone points; also harpoons with notches on one side). Local inhabitants were also farmers (they cultivated millet, like their counterparts in Northern China) and stock-breeders (rearing cattle and, possibly, horse).

Their rectangular wattle-and-daub semi-subterranean houses, as mentioned, were 30-40 sq. m. in size. Wooden houses were also found, similar to winter dwellings used by the Ainou people on the Kuril Islands in the early 20th century. As it seems, all these houses had neither doors nor windows, the only way of access being an aperture in the roof that was also used to remove the smoke, and the stairs consisting of an inclined tree trunk with incised steps. Similar structures were in use until recently in winter dwellings amongst various peoples in Manchuria and Siberia, as well as among the Koriaks in the Northern Pacific. For these peoples as well as for those of Alaska reported by Cook in the course of his third journey two centuries ago, such stairs had sacred connotations, and were viewed as the guards of the house.

Both Soviet-Mongolian digs and our own investigations have yielded a rich archaeological assemblage, that shed light on the early communities in Central Asia, who were hunters, fishers and food collectors, and, at the same time, sedentary farmers and stock-breeders.

7,000 years ago, the people in that presently forgotten area of Central Asia, took part in their own manner in the process of Neolithisation that encompassed the entire Eurasia. Adapting to a very special local environment, they chose an original form of food-producing economy, comparable to the broadly contemporaneous great civilizations of Yangshao and Longshan in China, Jomon in Japan, as well as those of southern Siberia, Kazakhstan, Central and Eastern Europe, and the European Early Neolithic complex (exemplified by the 'Linear pottery'), which extended from the Carpathian Mountains to Armorica. They were both hunter-gatherers and farmers. At present it is difficult to assess which branch of their economy played a leading role, this remains one of the main objectives of our project; we may only suggest that these branches were mutually complementary. In contrast to their predecessors, they were rather sedentary dwellers than nomads. And they remained so, until the new change of climate and the advance of the steppe made them to change their subsistence: they became again hunters and, more importantly, stock-breeders, who increasingly led the herds of goat, sheep, camels and horses still further behind the endless horizon.

Author's Address

Michel Louis SÉFÉRIADÈS
UMR 6566
CNRS, Université Rennes 1, Rennes 2 et Nantes,
Ministère de la Culture
Laboratoire d'Anthropologie, Université de Rennes 1,
Campus de Beaulieu
35042-Rennes Cédex, FRANCE
Email: michel.seferiades@univ-rennes1.fr

Bibliography

BERKELEY, C.P., NELSON, N.C., 1926: Geology and Prehistoric Archaeology of the Gobi Desert. *Am. Mus. Novit* (New York), vol. 222, p. 3-18.

CHANG, K.-C., 1986, *The Archaeology of Ancient China*, Yale University Press: Taiwan Edition.

DEREVIANKO, A.P., 1970, *Novopetrovskaja kul'tura Srednego Amura*. Novosibirsk.

DEREVIANKO, A.P., 1994, Central and Northern Asia during the Neolithic. In *History of Humanity, vol. I: Prehistory and Beginnings of Civilization*, edited by S.J. De Laet. Paris, Unesco, p. 457-467.

DEREVIANKO, A.P., DORJ, D, 1992, Neolithic Tribes in Northern Parts of Central Asia. In *History of Civilizations of Central Asia, vol. I*, edited by A.H. Dani, V.M. Masson. Paris, Unesco, p. 169-189.

DEREVIANKO, A.P., OLSEN, J.W., TSEVENDORJ, D., 1996, *Archaeological Studies carried out by the joint Russian-Mongolian-American Expedition in Mongolia in 1995*. Novosibirsk, 1996.

DEREVIANKO, A.P., OLSEN, J.W., TSEVENDORJ, D., 1998, *Archaeological Studies carried out by the joint Russian-Mongolian-American Expedition in Mongolia in 1996*. Novosibirsk, 1998.

DORJ, D., 1969, Neolithic Burials and Dwellings in Eastern Mongolia. *Izvestiya Akademii Nauk Mongol'skoy Narodnoy Respubliki*, p. 34-53.

DORJ, D. 1971, *Neolit vostocnoj Mongolii*. Ulaan Baatar.

DORJ, D., 1974, Tamsa-Bulagkaja kul'tura i eë mesto v drevnejshej istorii Tsentral'noj Azii. *Rol' kochevîkh narodov v Tsivilizatsii Tsentral'noj Azii*. Ulaan Baatar, p. 43-56.

DORJ, D., DEREVIANKO, A.P., 1970, Novîje materiali dlja izuchenija nêolita Vostochnoj Mongolii. *Izvestiya Akademii Nauk Mongol'skoy Narodnoy Respubliki*, Ulaan Baatar, p.43-56.

FAIRSERVIS, W.A. Jr., 1993, *Archaeology of the Southern Gobi of Mongolia*. Carolina Academic Press. Durham, North Carolina.

JOMON, 1998, *Jomon. L'art du Japon des Origines*. Maison de la Culture du Japon à Paris.

KIM, J.-H., 1978, *The Prehistory of Korea*. The University Press of Hawaii, Honolulu.

KILUNOVSKAYA, M., SEMENOV, V., 1995, *The Land of the Heart of Asia*, St Petersburg, Ego Publishers.

KYZLASOV, L.P., 1982, *Drevnjaja Tuva*. Moscow.

MILLEDGE NELSON, S., 1993, *The Archaeology of Korea*. Cambrige University Press.

MILLEDGE NELSON, S., 1995, *The Archaeology of Northeast China. Beyond the Great Wall*. Routledge, London.

NATSAGDORJ, S., 1987, *Archaeology, Ethnography and Anthropology of Mongolia*. Novosibirsk.

NAVAN, D., 1975, *The Bronze Age in Eastern Mongolia*. Ulan Bator.

NELSON, N.C., 1926a, The Dune Dwellers of the Gobi. *Natural History*, vol. 28, p. 305-308.

NELSON, N.C., 1926b. Prehistoric Archaeology of the Gobi Desert. *American Museum Novitates*, 222, p. 10-16.

NOVGORODOVA, E.A., 1989, *Drevniaia Mongolija*.. Moscow.

OKLADNIKOV, A.P. 1968. *Istorija Siberi. I. Drevnjaja Sibir'*. Léningrad.

OKLADNIKOV A.P., 1986, *Paleolit Mongolii*.. Novosibirsk.

OKLADNIKOV, A.P., DEREVIANKO, A.P. 1970, Tamsag-Bulak. Neoliticeskaja kul'tura Vostocnoj Mongolii. *Materialî po istorii i filologii Tsentral'noy Azii*, vol. 5, p. 3-20.

SEFERIADES, M., 1993, The European Neolithisation Process. *Porocilo o razskovanju paleolita, neolita in eneolita v Sloveniji* 21, Ljubljana, p. 137-162.

SEFERIADES, M., 1999, A Tamsagbulag, les Premiers Paysans de Mongolie. *Archéologia* (Dijon) 354, mars, p. 56-65.

SEFERIADES, M., 2000, In the Heart of the Eurasian Steppe: Ancient Hunter-Gatherers, First Sedentary Farmers and Nomad Stock Herders of Mongolia (8000-3000 BC). In *Late Prehistoric Exploitation of the Eurasian Steppe. Papers presented for the Symposium to be held 12 Jan-16 Jan 2000*, edited by C. Renfrew and M. Levine. The McDonald Institute for Archaeological Research, Cambridge, Vol. III, p. 107-125.

SEFERIADES, M., STANKO, V., 2000, Simples Gibiers ou Objets de Culte? Les Bisons Préhistoriques d'Anetovka (Ukraine), *Archéologia (Dijon)* 370, p. 50-55.

VASILEVSKIJ, R.S., 1985, *Ancient Cultures of Mongolia*. Novosibirsk.

SKELETAL MARKERS OF TASK ACTIVITIES IN IRON AGE HUMAN REMAINS FROM MISHRIFE (CENTRAL SYRIA)

Alessandro CANCI & Daniele MORANDI BONACOSSI (RAL SYRIA)

Résumé : Les fouilles entreprises à partir du 1999 par une mission mixte syrienne-française-allemande ont mis au jour un petit cimetière de l'Age du Fer II. Les tombes faisaient partie d'un niveau situé entre deux horizons d'occupation, chaque un caractérisé par la présence de fosses, de greniers et de terrains en plein air doués de matériaux pour le travail et la conservation des céréales et des olives (mortiers, pilons, meules, silos, jarres). Ces terrains probablement étaient las cours des fermes d'un grand village rural du VIIIème siècle AD. Dans le cimetière ont a trouvés six squelettes complets et bien conservés, qui appartenaient à six adultes des deux sexes. Malgré l'échantillon petit, le bon état de conservation des squelettes a permis d'obtenir des informations pour la reconstitution du style de vie dans une communauté rurale de l'Age du Fer II. Les modifications observées au niveau des membres supérieurs suggèrent une activité intense et répétée du bras et de l'avant-bras, compatible avec le travail de piochage, de mouture des céréales et avec la récolte des fruits ou des olives. L'analyse du tronc et des membres inférieurs a révélé la présence de compression vertébrale et hypertrophie des muscles adducteurs et fessiers. Ces modifications semblant suggérer des mouvements de la position à genoux a celle levée, effectués avec des poids sur la tête ou sur le dos. En conclusion, les marqueurs squelettiques observés dans le cimetière de Mišrife semblent être compatibles avec une activité de subsistance fondée sur l'agriculture. Cette interprétation est donc en accord avec le style de vie proposé pour la même communauté sur la base des évidences archéologiques.

Abstract: Excavations carried out since 1999 by a joint Syrian-Italian-German expedition at Tell Mishrife, ancient Qatna (Central Syria), brought to light a small Iron Age II inhumation cemetery. The graves belonged to a level interposed between two occupation horizons characterised by the presence of dwellings, granaries, and open-air areas equipped with installations for work (benches, mortars, grinding stones, pestles) and the preliminary storing of cereals and olives (silos and jars embedded in the trodden floors). These outdoor spaces were probably courtyards and threshing floors belonging to the farmsteads of a large rural village of the eighth century BC. The human remains of the cemetery consisted in six complete and well-preserved skeletons of adults of both sexes. In spite of the small sample size, the good state of preservation of the skeletons allowed us to obtain useful information for the reconstruction of the life style in a rural community of the Iron Age II. The changes observed on the upper limbs suggest strong and repetitive movements of the arm and the forearm compatible with the action of hoeing in the field, grinding the cereals in mortars and picking fruit or olives. In the trunk and the lower limbs, the vertebral compression, the robustness of hamstrings and adductor muscles, the presence of sacral and metatarsal accessory facets seem to suggest movements from squatting to standing position with heavy loads carried on the back or above the head. In conclusion, the skeletal markers observed seem to be compatible with a subsistence activity based on agriculture, thus supporting the interpretation of the Iron Age II occupation of Tell Mishrife proposed on the bases of the archaeological evidence.

INTRODUCTION

The excavation of Tell Mishrife, which is identified with the important Old and Middle Syrian city of Qatna (Du Mesnil du Buisson 1927), is a joint archaeological expedition carried out by the Directorate General of Antiquities and Museums of Syria, the University of Udine (Italy) and the University of Tübingen (Germany).

Qatna was, besides Aleppo and Mari, the major Syrian kingdom and commercial centre during the Old Syrian Period, from around 1900 to 1500 BC (Fig. 1)[1] Qatna's location at the crossroads between the main North-South route from Anatolia to Palestine and Egypt and the important East-West route from Mesopotamia through the Syrian Desert to the Mediterranean shore was the basis for its outstanding commercial, strategic, and political importantce.[2]

Tell Mishrife is still nowadays an impressive site located 18 km north-east of the modern city of Homs, in a large fertile plain at the interface between the dry steppe of the Palmyra region and the nearby Orontes valley (Wirth 1971, 391 ff.). A ditch and monumental ramparts almost perfectly square surround the site. Four city gates cut through the city walls, one in the middle of each side.

Previous archaeological work on Tell Mishrife was carried out by the French Count R. du Mesnil du Buisson from 1924 to 1929 (1926; 1927; 1928; 1930; 1935) and by a Syrian Expedition from 1994 to 1998 directed by Michel Al-Maqdissi (1996; 1997). During the excavations of the new international co-operation project, which started in 1999 and is directed by M. Al-Maqdissi, P. Pfälzner, and D. Morandi Bonacossi (Al-Maqdissi, Luciani, Morandi Bonacossi, Novák, Pfälzner eds. in print),[3] on the summit of the central mound a small inhumation cemetery of the Iron Age II (mid-ninth-eighth centuries BC) with six adult interments was discovered (Fig. 2). Two different grave typologies are attested:

- Simple earth inhumations (Tombs 7-8 and 11) and

- Interments in pits with a mud-brick covering consisting of a course of mud-bricks obliquely placed on end and leaning on the fill of the burial pit that had been

---

[1] For the political role of Qatna, see Klengel 2000; furthermore Helck 1971, Klengel 1992 and 1997, Kühne 1982.

[2] For the trade route through the Syrian Desert, see Klengel 1997, 365 f., Ismail 1996, 129 f., Abdallah 1996, 131 ff. and Mar'i 1996, 137. The journey from the Euphrates (Terqa) to Qatna lasted 10 days as in Mari letter ARM I 66 (Dossin 1950, 126-127); see also Mar'1 1996, 137, and Klengel 2000.

[3] Scientific responsibility of the project is shared with M. Luciani and M. Novák.

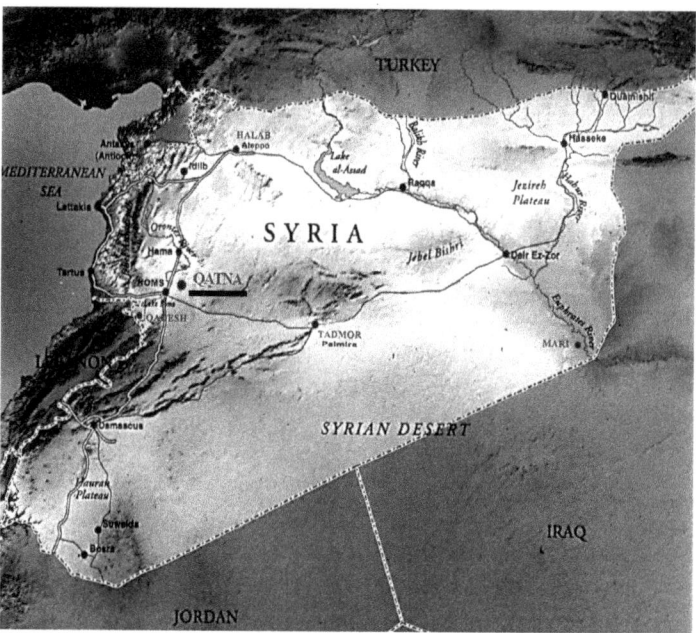

Figure 1. Geographical location of Mishrife, ancient Qatna.

strengthened on the top with mud plaster (Graves 2, 5, and 6). No exact comparison to this grave type is known so far from Iron Age Syria.

It is interesting to remark that while the Iron Age II graveyard at Mishrife consists exclusively of inhumation burials, the main contemporary cemeteries of Syria[4] are all characterised by cremation burials.

The bodies, which were found in a very good state of preservation, were lying on their right side with extended or slightly flexed legs. The hands were usually joined together on the pelvis; the cadavers had an E-W or ENE-WSW orientation and were facing S or SE.

The absolute lack of grave goods and the small number of excavated graves make it difficult to determine the existence of demographic status or ascribed ranking differentiations within the cemetery. However, the fact that three graves were simple inhumations in earth pits while three had a mud-brick covering might be interpreted as a possible indication of the existence of some kind of differentiation among the buried individuals.

Furthermore, in the case of Graves 2 and 5 evidence of a possible funerary ritual has been recognised. Directly on the top of the fill of Grave 2 an ash lens and a crushed jar were discovered. A similar ash layer was found also on top of the fill of Grave 5. Further, a trapezoid pierced basalt stone in secondary re-use (possibly a weight) was horizontally embedded from the top of the grave in the grave fill immediately to the south of the mud-brick covering of the tomb, i.e. to the south of the body.

Sex determination (cf. *infra*) has shown that all the graves with mud-brick covering contained bodies of female individuals, while in the simple interments males were buried. Hence, tomb type seems to be associated with demographic status. Finally, possible consanguinity-affiliation is indicated by recurrent anatomical variations occurring on the skeletons. This hypothesis, together with the fact that the burials are distributed over a very localised area, are not numerous, and cover a rather short time span, might indicate that the cemetery was a small graveyard reserved to a kinship-group (endogamic group).

Summing up, the Iron Age II inhumation cemetery at Mishrife represents a striking anomaly within the general context of the contemporary western Syrian cemeteries, which are dominated by cremation burials. It is not clear so far if this has to be considered a local cultural feature or has to be related to ranking differences among the individuals buried in these cemeteries or rather to the fact that the graves on the summit of the central mound at Mishrife belong to what seems to be a small "family" graveyard rather than a larger public cemetery.

METHODS

The human remains consisted in complete and well-preserved skeletons belonged to 3 adult males and 3 adult females from burials dated to Iron Age II.

Sexing was done using morphological cranial and pelvis traits (Ferembach *et al.* 1979) and univariate and multivariate techniques based on metric traits as reported by Borgognini and Pacciani (1993); age at death was estimated on the basis of dental wear, exo- and endocranial suture closure, pubic symphysis surface and developmental stages of the dentition and epiphyseal union of various parts of the skeleton (Brothwell 1981; Ubelaker 1989). Stature was

---

[4] Such as e.g. that of Periods III-IV discovered at the near site of Hama (Riis 1948), the forst cemetery of Deve Höyük (Moorey 1980), the burials of the cemeteries of Yunus (Woolley 1914), Tell Shiukh Fawqani, Area H (Bahlul, Barro, D'alfonso n.d.) and Ras el-Bassit (Courbin 1993), and the graves found at Tell Arqa (Thalmann 1978, 73, 77). For an overview, cf. also Bienkowski 1982.

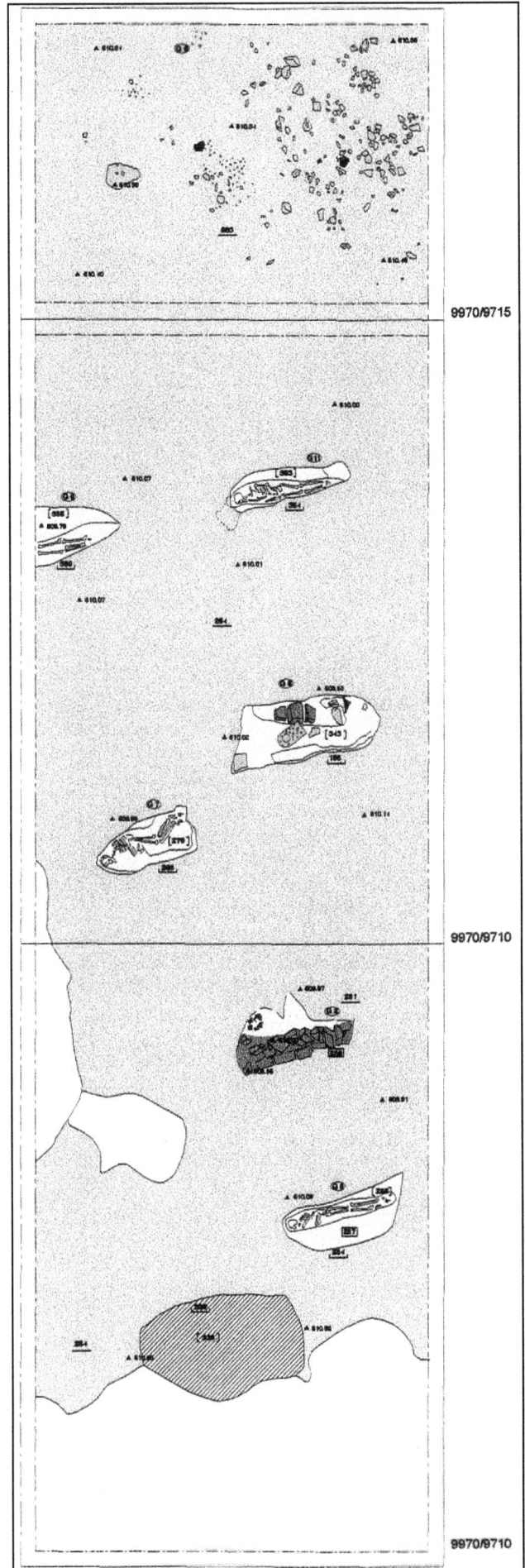

Figure 2. Plan of Iron Age II cemetery at Mishrife.

evaluated using the formulae of Trotter and Gleser (1952) for blacks and palaeopathological diagnosis were made following the criteria of Ortner and Putschar (1985), Resnick (1995) and Capasso *et al.* (1999).

RESULTS AND DISCUSSION

In spite the small number of the human sample, the integrity of the whole of the skeletal components allowed us to obtain useful data for the reconstruction of the lifestyle during the Iron Age.

Skeletons showed short stature with average values of 161.4 cm (range 157.6 cm - 167.6 cm) and of 152.4 cm (range 147.9 cm - 158.6 cm) for men and women respectively; age at death of both sexes was about 37 years.

The skulls were dolichocranic and the postcranial bones exhibited a gracile shape but marked muscular insertions were present. The lower limbs of both sexes showed absence of platymeria and platycnemia indicating moderate activity of the muscles of the legs. This evidence could be related to reduced mobility on the territory (Angel 1966).

The 50% of the subjects showed anatomical variations related to anomalies of the development of inherited origin consisting in non-union of the posterior arch in the atlas, a "dinner-fork" rib and a partial sacralization of the fifth lumbar vertebra (Fig. 3). According to Barnes (1994) the high prevalence in the sample of these inherited anomalies could be suggestive of endogamy in the group (kinship relations) although the negative effect on foetus of environmental factors (nutritional, mechanical, infective, etc.) cannot fully excluded.

The oral health was very poor. The 80% of the individuals showed conspicuous and serious *ante mortem* tooth loss (three subjects at time of death were almost completely edentulous); caries and abscess were observed on the 40% of the sample.

The degree of alveolar reabsorption was high in all the dentitions examined (Fig. 4). This evidence could explain the loss of the teeth during the life. As a matter of fact, the poor horal hygiene could create the conditions for the proliferation of the bacteria infecting the parodontal tissue and subsequent alveolar reabsorption and tooth loss.

Enamel defects and hypocalcifications were observable on teeth of all subjects indicating diffusion of aspecific stress episodes in infancy (Fig. 4). No signs of specific infections (e.g. tuberculosis, brucellosis etc.) were observed on the skeletons. Periostitis affected the tibial diaphyses of two individuals indicating aspecific infection or traumatic consequence.

The vertebral columns showed signs biomechanical stress resulting in avulsion fractures of vertebral endplates, following strong hyperdorsiflexion of the trunk, or in compression fractures of the vertebral bodies due to recurrent movements of spinal flexion and lateral bending.

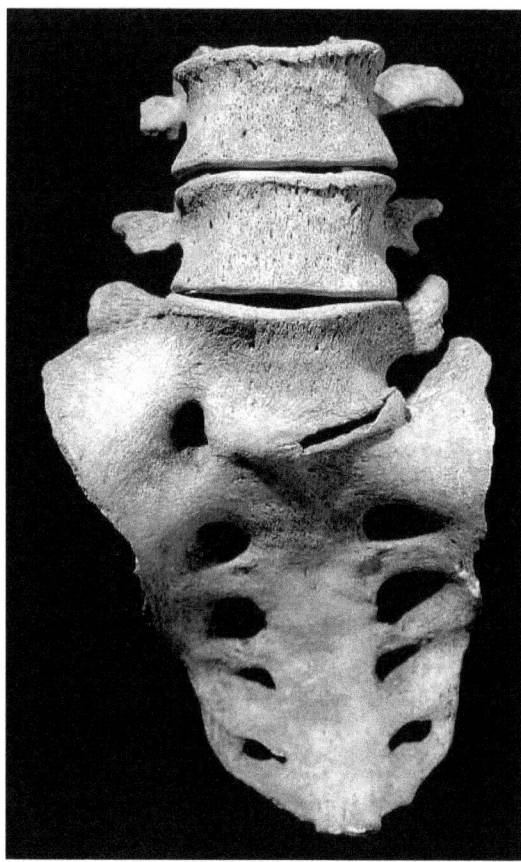

Figure 3. Incomplete sacralization of fifth lumbar vertebra resulting in scoliosis in a male from the Iron Age II cemetery at Mishrife.

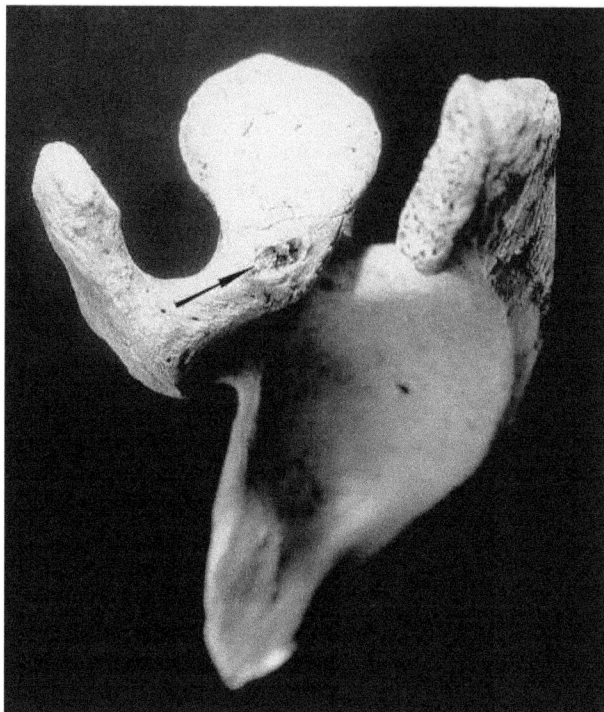

Figure 5. Supraglenoid articular facet (arrow) on the right scapula of a male from the Iron Age II cemetery at Mishrife. This feature is consequence of repetitive abduction of the arms above shoulder height.

These alterations are compatible with frequent carrying of heavy loads on the back.

The scapular girdle showed strong changes due to abduction/elevation movements resulting in erosion of acromioclavicular joint and supraglenoid articular facet (Wienker and Wood 1988) (Fig. 5). The upper limbs of the 67% of the subjects showed the so-called "Hill Sachs lesion", an uncommon dislocation of humeral head against the scapula (Hill and Sachs 1940) and marked enthesopaties at the insertions of extensors and flexors muscles on the forearms.

A case of traumatic avulsion of the right radial tuberosity and compression and erosion of the capitular surface involving a woman was observable. On this subject, it is interesting to remark that rupture of the distal tendon of the biceps muscle is a rare occurrence following biomechanical stress by high-tensile force repeatedly exerted by muscle contraction (Oikawa and Narama 1998).

The 33% of individuals showed marked osteoarthritic changes of the femoral condyles (Fig. 6) and tibial plateau consisting in osteophytosis, roughening, pitting at the joint surfaces (Rogers and Waldron 1995). Furthermore, the 83% of the skeletons exhibited, remodelling of greater trochanter and rotation and flattening of lesser trochanter on the femur.

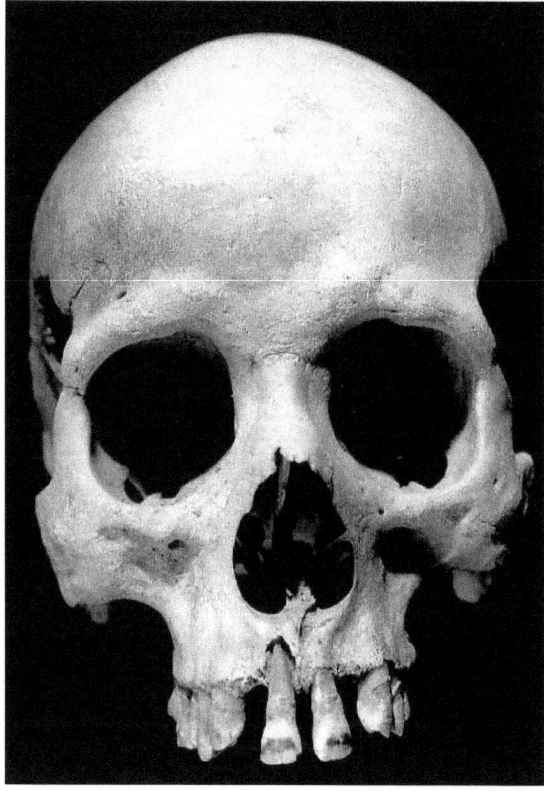

Figure 4. Male calvarium from the Iron Age II cemetery at Mishrife showing stains of hypocalcification and marked exposure of teeth roots subsequent to severe alveolar reabsorption.

The 67% of the subjects showed bone spurs consequence of inflammation of the Achilles tendon on calcaneum and at last, of the skeletons kneeling accessory facets were present on the 33% of the first metatarsals.

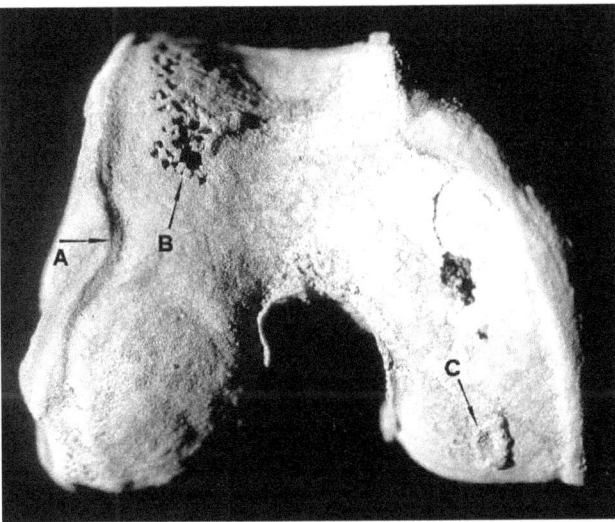

Figure 6. Condyles of the right femur of a male from the Iron Age II cemetery at Mishrife showing severe osteoarthritic changes consisting in marginal lipping (arrow A), erosion (arrow B) and osteophytes (arrow C) on the articular surface.

CONCLUSIONS

The whole of alterations observed on upper limbs suggest that the dynamics of movements consisted mainly in abduction, elevation, circumduction and depression of the arm and strong extension and supination of the forearm compatible with the action of hoeing in the field, grinding the grain in mortars or in quern and picking fruit or olives (Capasso et al. 1999).

In the lower limbs the high prevalence of alterations at the knee joints, the robustness of adductors and the hamstrings, the tendinitis at calcaneum and the kneeling accessory facets seems suggests movements from a squatting to a standing up position with heavy loads carried on the back or above the head (Ubelaker 1979; Molleson 1989).

Summarizing, the anthropological study on human remains from Iron Age II levels pointed out the following conclusions:

1) The diffusion on the skeletons of several developmental field defects of inherited origin suggesting endogamy;

2) High prevalence in both sexes of biomechanical stress resulting in degenerative osteoarthrosis and traumas;

3) High prevalence in both sexes of dental indicators of stress indicating poor health conditions during infancy.

The whole of these results seems to be compatible with a picture of a likely kinship group of low social status with a subsistence activity based on agriculture. The work was hard in terms of physical demand and probably required many hours a day to be accomplished.

Acknowledgments

Research grants by MIUR Cofin. 2001, MAE 2001, Cariverona Foundation 2001, University of Udine.

Authors' Addresses

Alessandro CANCI
Unit of Anthropology
Dept. of Ethology, Ecology and Evolution
University of Pisa
via Santa Maria 55
56126 Pisa ITALY

Daniele MORANDI BONACOSSI
Dept. of History and Conservation of Cultural Heritage
University of Udine
via Antonini 8
33100 Udine ITALY

Bibliography

ABDALLAH F., 1996, Palmyre dans le Complex économico-politique du XVIIIe Siècle av. J.-C. *Les Annales Archéologiques Arabes Syriennes*, 42, pp. 131-135.

ANGEL L., 1966, *Early skeletons from Tranquillity*, California. Washington D.C.: Smithsonian Institution Press.

AL-BAHLUL KH., BARRO A., D'ALFONSO L., n.d., Area H. The Iron Age Cremation Cemetery, L. Bachelot / F.M. Fales (eds.), *Tell Shioukh Fawqani (1994-1998)*. Beirut.

BARNES E., 1994, *Developmental defects of the axial skeleton in paleopathology*. Niwot: University Press of Colorado.

BIENKOWSKI P., 1982, Some Remarks on the Practice of Cremation in the Levant. *Levant* 14, pp. 80-89.

BORGOGNINI TARLI S.M., & PACCIANI E., 1993, *I resti umani nello scavo archeologico. Metodiche di recupero e studio*. Rome: Bulzoni Ed.

BROTHWELL D., 1981, *Digging up bones*. Oxford: Oxford University Press.

CAPASSO L., KENNEDY K.A.R., & WILCZACK C.A., 1999, *Atlas of occupational markers on human remains*. Teramo: Edigrafital.

COURBIN P., 1993, *Fouilles de Bassit. Tombes du Fer*. Paris.

DOSSIN G., 1950, *Correspondance de Šamši-Addu et de ses fils*. Paris.

DU MESNIL DU BUISSON R., 1926, Les Ruines de'el-Mishrifé au Nord-Est de Homs. Première Campagne de Fouilles 1924. *Syria* 7, pp. 1-59.

DU MESNIL DU BUISSON R., 1927, L'Ancienne Qatna ou les Ruines de'el-Mishrifé. Deuxième Campagne de Fouilles 1927 (1e article). *Syria* 8, pp. 227-301.

DU MESNIL DU BUISSON R., 1928, L'Ancienne Qatna ou les Ruines de'el-Mishrifé. Deuxième Campagne de Fouilles 1927 (2e et 3e article). *Syria* 9, pp. 6-24 and pp. 81-89.

DU MESNIL DU BUISSON R., 1930, Comte rendu de la Quatrième Campagne de Fouilles a Mishrifé-Qatna 1929. *Syria* 11, pp. 146-163.

DU MESNIL DU BUISSON R., 1935, *Le Site archeologique de Mishrife-Qatna*. Paris.

FEREMBACH D., SCWIDETZKY I., & STLOUKAL M., 1979, Recommandations pour déterminer l'age et le sexe sur le squelette. *Bullettins et Mémoires de la Société d'Anthropologie de Paris* 6, pp. 7-45.

HELCK W., 1971, *Die Beziehungen Ägyptens zu Vorderasien im 3. und 2. Jahrtausend v.Chr.* 2nd edition, first published 1962. Wiesbaden.

HILL H.A., & SACHS M.D., 1940, The grooved defect of the humeral head. *Radiology*, 35, pp. 690-700.

ISMAIL F., 1996, Qatna (Tell Mischrife) in den altbabylonischen Dokumenten, *Les Annales Archéologiques Arabes Syriennes*, 42, pp. 129-130.

KLENGEL H., 1992, *Syria 3000 to 300 BC.* Berlin.

KLENGEL H., 1997, Die historische Rolle der Stadt Aleppo im vorantiken Syrien, G. Wilhelm (ed.), *Die orientalische Stadt* (Colloquien der Deutschen Orient-Gesellschaft 1), 359-374.

KLENGEL H., 2000, Qatna 1999 – Ein historischer Überblick. *Mitteilungen der Deutschen Orient-Gesellschaft* 132, pp. 239-252.

KÜHNE C., 1982, Politische Szenerie und internationale Beziehungen Vorderasiens um die Mitte des 2. Jtd., H. Nissen / J. Renger (eds.), *Mesopotamien und seine Nachbarn* (Berliner Beiträge zum Vorderen Orient 1), 203-264. Berlin.

MAR'I A., 1996, Palmyra as an important Station on the Caravan's Road during the Second Millennium BC, *Les Annales Archéologiques Arabes Syriennes* 42, p. 137.

AL-MAQDISSI M., 1996, Reprise des fouilles à Mishrifeh en 1994. *Akkadica*, 99-100, 1-14.

AL-MAQDISSI M., 1997, Mishrifeh/Qatna. H. Weiss, Archaeology in Syria, *American Journal of Archaeology* 101, pp. 132-33.

MOLLESON T., 1989, Seed preparation in the Mesolithic: the osteological evidence. *Antiquity*, 63, pp. 356-362.

MOOREY P.R.S., 1980, *Cemeteries of the First Millennium BC. at Deve Höyük*, Oxford: B.A.R..

OIKAWA M., & NARAMA I., 1998, Enthesopathy of the radial tuberosity in two thoroughbred racehorses. *Journal of Comparative Pathology*, 118, pp. 135-143.

ORTNER D.J., & PUTSCHAR W.G.J., 1985, *Identification of pathological conditions in human skeletal remains.* Washington D.C.: Smithsonian Institution Press.

RESNICK D., 1995, *Diagnosis of bone and joint disorders.* Philadelphia: Saunders Company.

RIIS P.J., 1948, *Les cimetières à crémation. Hama. Fouilles et recherches de la Fondation Carlsberg 1931-1938, II. 3*, Copenhagen.

ROGERS J., & WALDRON T., 1995, *A field guide to joint disease in archaeology.* Chichester: Wiley.

THALMANN J.P., 1978, Tell 'Arqa, Campagnes I-III (1972-1974), *Syria* 55, 1-152.

TROTTER M., & GLESER G.C., 1952, Estimation of stature from long bones of American Whites and Negroes. *American Journal of Physical Anthropology*, 10, pp. 463-514.

UBELAKER D.H., 1979, Skeletal evidence for kneeling in prehistoric Ecuador. *American Journal of Physical Anthropology*, 51, pp. 679-686.

UBELAKER D.H., 1989, *Human skeletal remains. Excavation, analysis, interpretation.* Washington D.C.: Taraxacum.

WIENKER C.W., & WOOD J.E., 1988, Osteological individuality indicative of migrant citrus laboring. *Journal of Forensic Sciences*, 33, pp. 562-567.

WIRTH E., 1971, *Syrien. Eine geographische Landeskunde.* Darmstadt.

WOOLLEY C.L., 1914, Hittite Burial Customs. *Liverpool Annals of Archaeology and Anthropology* 6, pp. 87-98.

LE PREMIER PEUPLEMENT DE LA NOUVELLE-CALEDONIE : POTERIES LAPITA ET SOCIETES OCEANIENNES COLONISATRICES

Christophe SAND, Jacques BOLE & André OUETCHO

Résumé : Au cours des cinq dernières années l'image des modalités d'expansion de l'Ensemble Culturel Lapita, qui caractérise la première arrivée de l'homme en Océanie lointaine (sud des îles Salomons), a été profondément redéfinie. Cet article propose une synthèse des nouvelles données obtenues dans le sud de la Mélanésie, en focalisant le sujet sur la Nouvelle-Calédonie, avec la présentation des remarquables poteries décorées caractéristiques du Lapita. L'analyse des résultats montre une logique dans les différenciations qui apparaissent dans l'ensemble culturel au fur et à mesure de son expansion sur un espace maritime de plus de 4000 km, entre 1200 et 850 avant J.C. Ceci permet d'émettre des hypothèses plus fondées sur les modalités du premier peuplement austronésien du Pacifique sud-ouest et ses évolutions.

Abstract: During the last five years, the understanding of the expansion process of the Lapita Cultural Complex, which characterizes the first arrival of humans in Remote Oceania (south of the Solomons), has been deeply refined. This paper proposes a synthesis of the new data from southern Melanesia, focusing on New Caledonia, with the presentation of the spectacular decorated pots that characterize Lapita. The analysis of the results shows a logical differentiation in the Cultural Complex during its expansion over a maritime region of over 4000 km, between 1200 BC and 850 BC. This allows for more structured hypothesis on the modalities of first Austronesian settlement in the south-western Pacific and it's evolutions.

INTRODUCTION GENERALE

Au cours du dernier demi-siècle, une bonne partie des recherches préhistoriques menées dans le Pacifique Sud-Ouest a focalisé sur la fouille de sites renfermant un type de poterie appelé Lapita, caractérisé par des décors pointillés et reconnu comme le témoin matériel d'une ancienne communauté culturelle enjambant il y a environ 3000 ans la division ethnographique entre la Mélanésie et la Polynésie (Golson 1971). Les études ont permis l'identification archéologique d'un "Ensemble Culturel Lapita" dépassant la poterie, qu'il est possible de lier clairement à l'avancée d'un front de colonisation humaine en Mélanésie du Sud et en Polynésie occidentale (Green 1979). Ce peuplement par des groupes de langue austro-nésienne, représente la plus ancienne arrivée de l'homme dans cette région culturelle appelée l'Océanie lointaine et une des avancées colonisatrices les plus rapides de la préhistoire mondiale (Kirch 1997).

La Nouvelle-Calédonie, archipel du sud de la Mélanésie riche en sites de cette tradition culturelle, occupe une place particulière dans l'étude du phénomène Lapita. Le nom de la tradition céramique vient d'un site de la Grande Terre calédonienne, le premier daté au début des années 1950 (Gifford et Shutler 1956). Afin de mieux définir le Lapita calédonien dans son cadre régional, le Département Archéologie de Nouvelle-Calédonie a débuté au milieu des années 1990 un programme d'envergure sur cette période (Sand 1996). Cet article souhaite présenter les principaux résultats obtenus, en focalisant l'attention sur les données chronologiques et sur la diversité de l'ensemble céramique Lapita, avant d'aborder rapidement les contraintes culturelles de sociétés colonisatrices insulaires océaniennes.

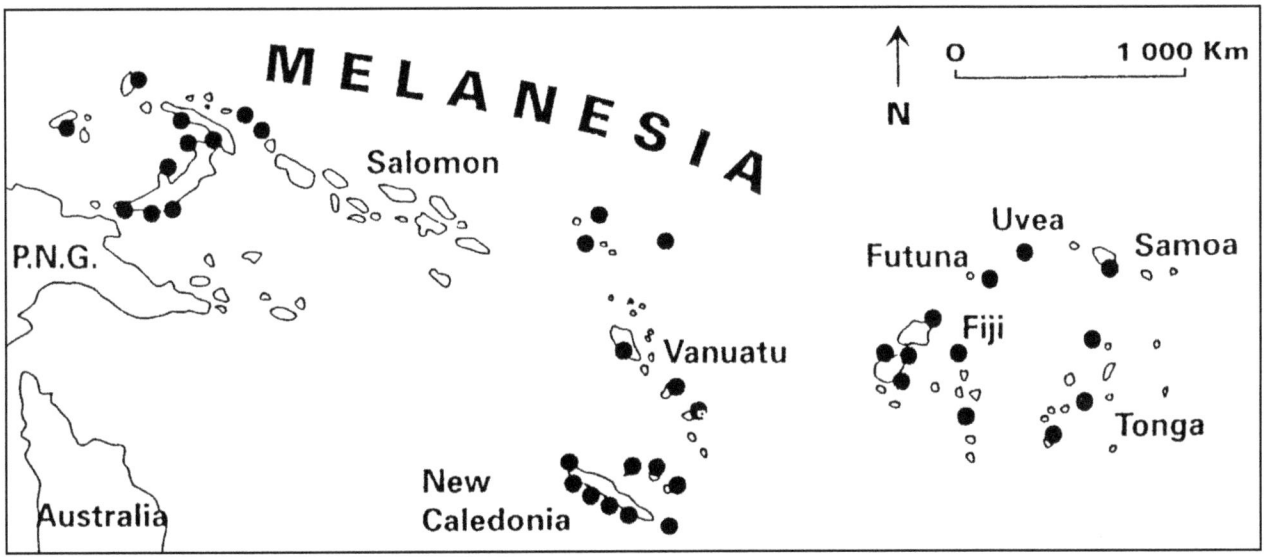

Figure 1. Localisation des différents archipels et des principaux sites Lapita du Pacifique sud-ouest.

CADRE GEOGRAPHIQUE ET CHRONOLOGIQUE

Le Pacifique sud-ouest (fig. 1), d'une longueur maximale de 4500 km, est formé des îles situées à l'est de la Nouvelle-Guinée et de l'Australie, comprenant du nord-ouest à l'est les archipels mélanésiens insulaires et les archipels de la Polynésie occidentale. La Nouvelle-Calédonie, localisée au sud du croissant mélanésien, est formée d'une Grande Terre d'origine continentale mesurant plus de 400km de longueur, ainsi que de nombreuses îles de nature corallienne.

Le nord de la Mélanésie insulaire a été peuplé il y a plus de 30000 ans (Kirch 2000). Les données archéologiques disponibles à ce jour ne permettent pas de démontrer la présence de ce peuplement pré-céramique au Vanuatu et en Nouvelle-Calédonie. L'apparition de poteries décorées de motifs pointillés géométriques qui caractérisent le Lapita, est datée d'environ 1500-1300 avant J.C. dans l'archipel de Bismarck, à l'est de la Nouvelle-Guinée, correspondant à l'arrivée dans la région de nouveaux groupes culturels originaires d'Asie du Sud-Est (Kirch 2001). Le premier peuplement humain dans le carrefour géographique que représente l'archipel des Reef/Santa-Cruz entre les îles Salomon et le Vanuatu, est daté autours de 1200-1100 avant J.C. (Green 1991). De cette région, des groupes sont partis vers le sud et l'est, atteignant la Polynésie occidentale vers 900 avant J.C. (Burley et Dickinson 2001). D'après les données de plus de 80 nouvelles datations, réalisées au cours des dernières années principalement par AMS, le peuplement de l'archipel calédonien débute vers 1100-1050 avant J.C. (Sand 1997a). Les études stratigraphiques montrent une permanence des occupations sur plusieurs générations, avec une poursuite de la fabrication de poteries Lapita jusqu'à environ 800-750 avant J.C., puis une chronologie céramique marquée par des poteries imprimées au battoir, incisées et décorées au coquillage (Sand 1999).

Nos travaux indiquent donc que la chronologie de fabrication des poteries Lapita en Nouvelle-Calédonie est limitée à moins de trois siècles. Ceci est une conclusion majeure (Sand 2000a), puisque les synthèses réalisées durant les vingt dernières années indiquaient une perduration du phénomène Lapita sur environ 1500 ans (Galipaud 1996 ; Frimigacci 1999). Cette courte période "Lapita" identifiée en Nouvelle-Calédonie, qui rejoint celles définies récemment pour le Vanuatu (Bedford 2000), Fidji (Anderson et Clark 1999) et la Polynésie occidentale (Burley *et al.* 1999 ; Sand 2000b), permet d'analyser de façon totalement nouvelle la représentativité de la tradition céramique pointillée (Sand 2001).

LA VARIETE DU LAPITA DE NOUVELLE-CALEDONIE

La Nouvelle-Calédonie a le privilège d'être l'archipel océanien où le plus de tessons bien conservés de poteries Lapita ont été découverts à ce jour, permettant une analyse sur un nombre significatif de vestiges (Sand 1997b). Une rapide description de cette tradition est proposée ici, en analysant tout d'abord les variations des formes typologiques, ensuite les principaux motifs décoratifs pointillés et enfin les ensembles de composants minéralogiques (voir Sand 1996).

Les formes céramiques Lapita : Une des caractéristiques majeures de la tradition Lapita est la complexité des formes typologiques identifiées (fig. 2). La majorité des bords est sortant, avec un méplat. Parfois la forme est composite, un bandeau d'argile vertical étant alors ajouté dans le prolongement du corps du pot.

La principale forme typologique identifiée est celle du pot à encolure droite ou faiblement sortante, limitée par un épaulement plus ou moins marqué puis par une carène. La taille de ces pots carénés s'échelonne entre 15cm et plus de 60cm. La seconde catégorie majeure de forme céramique Lapita est composée de plats, parfois fixés sur un pied. Les pieds ont des diamètres très variables: certains sont simplement formés d'un cylindre plein ou creux, alors que d'autres ont une forme évasée. Il reste à signaler la présence de couvercles posés sur des bords composites, de poteries à bord rentrant, de forme arrondie, ainsi que de socles en forme de cylindre, pour poser des pots.

Les motifs décoratifs : L'identification d'un ensemble céramique régional s'étendant sur plusieurs milliers de kilomètres à travers le Pacifique Sud-Ouest a été possible avant tout grâce aux décors pointillés stylistiquement proches découverts des îles Bismarck à la Nouvelle-Calédonie et à la Polynésie occidentale (fig. 3). La structuration du décor Lapita est divisée en un ensemble de frises comportant de nombreuses variations, limitant un bandeau central comportant le motif principal (Siorat 1990). L'analyse des grandes classes de décors du bandeau central identifiées dans le Lapita calédonien montre que les constructions géométriques primaires sont peu nombreuses, avec l'identification d'une dizaine de grandes catégories de motifs (fig. 4). Le motif du labyrinthe est probablement la construction géométrique la plus complexe. Les autres catégories principales sont les motifs ondulés, les triangles emboîtés et les rectangles se divisant en triangles, qui sont les constructions géométriques les plus simples mais également celles où le plus de variations sont possibles. La multiplication des fouilles en Mélanésie a permis d'identifier dans l'ensemble décoratif Lapita la présence de visages humains plus ou moins stylisés. L'ensemble calédonien le plus complexe est celui de la double face, avec un décor comprenant, enveloppé dans un cadre arrondi, une forme humaine stylisée, avec une tête allongée et des bras terminés en spirale, ainsi qu'un corps en triangle qui forme un second visage. La majorité des visages en triangle ne comportent néanmoins pas de motif anthropomorphe supérieur. Le motif de la face simple est caractérisé par la présence d'un visage avec le nez et les yeux, limité par un médaillon. Les yeux sont formés par deux impressions en croissants, avec parfois une impression ronde au centre. La construction géométrique du visage allongé a donné lieu à une évolution stylistique variée. La disparition des médaillons aboutit à la formation d'un motif répétitif oeil-nez. L'abstraction finale est atteinte avec le remplacement de l'oeil par un motif géométrique (rectangle rempli, croix, point etc.). Des tessons de poteries décorées par d'autres techniques (incisions, impressions au battoir ou cardiales)

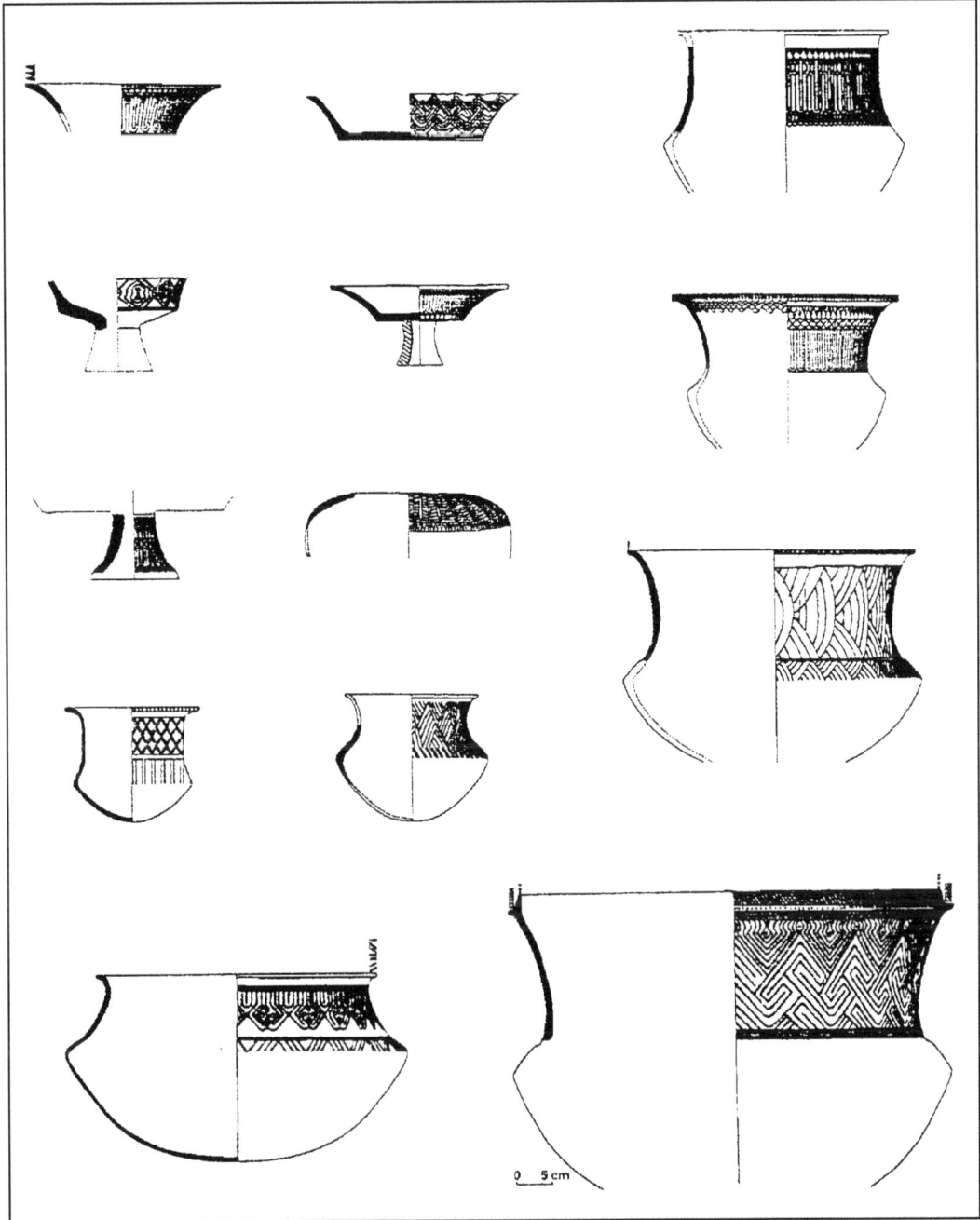

Figure 2. Variété des formes céramiques Lapita de Nouvelle-Calédonie.

ont été découverts dans tous les sites où se trouvaient des poteries décorées de pointillés. La proportion de décors incisés varie par exemple entre 10% et 20%. L'inventaire des motifs décoratifs incisés montre l'existence d'un nombre restreint de formes céramiques et de motifs.

Les composants minéralogiques : Depuis longtemps, les archéologues ont noté la présence répétée de grandes proportions de dégraissant corallien dans les tessons Lapita. L'avantage d'être un produit facilement disponible sur chaque île pour des populations de navigateurs était contrebalancée par l'impossibilité de cuire les pots à haute température, aboutissant à des pots peu solides, souvent poreux et ne pouvant pas avoir une fonction d'ustensile de cuisson. En parallèle à ces tessons fragiles, une partie des tessons associe du sable corallien et des éléments lithiques.

Enfin, certains tessons Lapita ne sont pas du tout dégraissés au sable corallien : ces poteries plus fines, solides et souvent de petite taille, caractérisent la fin de la période Lapita.

ANALYSE

Les premiers siècles de peuplement de la Nouvelle-Calédonie sont d'une importance centrale pour notre compréhension des évolutions locales des sociétés austronésiennes. Les découvreurs austronésiens s'installèrent de façon préférentielle à l'embouchure des rivières, face à des passes dans le récif corallien ou face à des accès faciles à la haute mer (Frimigacci 1980 ; Sand *et al.* 2002), avec une exploitation intensive, au début du peuplement, des

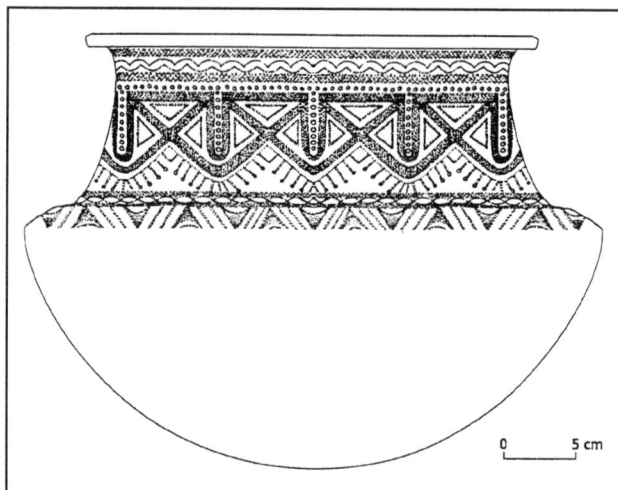

Figure 3. Exemple de reconstitution de poteries Lapita de Nouvelle-Calédonie, montrant les différents bandeaux de décors pointillés.

ressources disponibles en mer, en bord de rivage et dans les mangroves (poissons, coquillages, tortues) (Sand 2000a). L'implantation des premiers villages à proximité de zones où des sols de bonne qualité horticole sont présents, indique l'existence d'une forme primitive d'horticulture, une donnée confirmée indépendamment par les reconstitutions linguistiques (Kirch 1997 ; Ross et al. 1998). Enfin, une partie de la consommation alimentaire de ces colonisateurs reposait sur la chasse d'animaux endémiques, entraînant la disparition rapide de toute une partie des espèces locales (Balouet et Olson 1989).

Les hameaux, composés de cases implantées en arrière de plage, étaient formés au départ de groupes peu nombreux. Une organisation relativement complexe devait gérer les relations entre les familles : en effet, sans un contrôle sur la vitesse de reproduction des groupes, sur la transmission à chaque génération des techniques de navigation et de construction des pirogues, sans une organisation poussée des expéditions d'exploration des zones maritimes inconnues, la progression austronésienne à travers la Mélanésie et la Polynésie occidentale en quelques siècles, sur plus de 4000 km d'Océan, n'aurait pas été possible (Green 1997). De plus, un des principes essentiels pour la survie des petits groupes colonisateurs est le développement d'échanges réguliers avec des groupes alliés, permettant de renouveler le stock génétique et d'obtenir une aide en cas de catastrophe naturelle majeure. L'existence d'échanges inter-insulaires est démontrée archéologiquement par le transport de pots et de matières premières comme l'obsidienne sur des distances pouvant atteindre 3000 km (Green et Kirch 1997 ; Sand et Sheppard 2000).

Contrairement à ce qui a été longtemps pensé, les groupes austronésiens n'avaient pas une société statique, mais se sont au contraire rapidement adaptés à leur nouvel environnement, s'enracinant à l'archipel et maîtrisant ses spécificités. Ceci a entraîné des évolutions précoces de certaines caractéristiques socioculturelles majeures (Spriggs 1997 ; Bedford 2000 ; Kirch 2000). Dans ce contexte se pose de façon nouvelle l'utilité des céramiques Lapita,

Figure 4. Variété des décors pointillés Lapita de Nouvelle-Calédonie.

uniquement produites lors de la phase de première colonisation. Bien que cette question ne soit toujours pas résolue, les données archéologiques permettent d'avancer quelques faits (Summerhayes 2000). Une partie de ces poteries de nature non utilitaire étaient échangées, parfois sur des distances de plusieurs centaines de kilomètres, laissant à penser que ces pots fabriqués par des groupes culturels colonisateurs, rentraient dans une symbolique liant entre elles les familles austronésiennes éparpillées à travers les îles. Ceci expliquerait en partie la grande homogénéité des formes, des décors et des textures spécifiques du Lapita. P.V. Kirch (1997) a récemment proposé de voir dans les visages humains réalisés sur les pots, des figurations d'ancêtres. Une partie des poteries Lapita auraient été échangées entre des groupes appa-rentés, dans le cadre de rites sociaux ayant pour but de rappeler symboliquement les liens généalogiques ancestraux.

Cette symbolique aurait fonctionné durant quelques générations, avant que l'enracinement de chaque communauté à son terroir, favorisée par l'augmentation démographique engendrant la stabilité économique, n'ait progressivement entraîné le relâchement des échanges formalisés et la fin de la production de ces pots, remplacés par d'autres ensembles céramiques (Sand 1995 ; Bedford

2000). Les fabricants de la poterie Lapita n'ont ainsi pas "disparu" à la suite d'une nouvelle arrivée de population, ils ont simplement cessé de fabriquer des poteries aux décors pointillés complexes, qui avaient perdu leur raison d'être dans la société, car liées à une symbolique ne fonctionnant que dans la phase de colonisation insulaire austronésienne.

CONCLUSION

La situation sociale, culturelle, linguistique, démographique et politique des groupes austronésiens de Nouvelle-Calédonie s'est profondément transformée et diversifiée durant le premier millénaire de peuplement de l'archipel. A la fin de la période de production des poteries Lapita, moins de 300 ans après la découverte, les populations de la Grande Terre et des îles Loyauté étaient prêtes à développer leurs propres caractéristiques socioculturelles et leurs spécificités d'organisation (Sand 1999). Il apparaît de plus en plus que la mise en place de ces caractéristiques uniques à la Nouvelle-Calédonie a été variable dans les temps et l'espace, avant d'aboutir près de 2000 ans plus tard aux sociétés kanak connues à travers les textes des premiers navigateurs européens, démontrant un dynamisme historique inattendu des sociétés mélanésiennes (Sand 1995). Afin de reconstituer correctement cette chronologie préhistorique de 3000 ans, il faut impérativement mieux définir aujourd'hui les caractéristiques du tout début de cette histoire: le jour où, pour la première fois, un homme arrivant du nord a sauté d'une pirogue sur une plage de la Nouvelle-Calédonie, dépositaire d'un savoir ancestral partagé par des milliers de marins austronésiens à travers le Pacifique Sud-Ouest.

Remerciements

Les travaux du Département Archéologie du Service des Musées et du Patrimoine de Nouvelle-Calédonie sont menés pour le compte de la Province des îles Loyauté, de la Province Nord et de la Province Sud. Des crédits complémentaires pour le programme sur le Lapita calédonien ont été obtenus auprès de la Sous-Direction de l'Archéologie (Ministère de la Culture, Paris). La participation au congrès de l'UISPP à Liège a été possible grâce à l'accord délivré par le Gouvernement de la Nouvelle-Calédonie. Nos remerciements à ces différentes institutions, ainsi qu'aux propriétaires fonciers et aux autorités coutumières qui ont permis les fouilles sur les différents sites Lapita de Nouvelle-Calédonie.

Adresse des auteurs

Christophe SAND
Jacques BOLÉ
André OUETCHO
Département Archéologie
Musée de Nouvelle-Calédonie
BP: 2393, 98846 Nouméa
Nouvelle-Calédonie
Email (bureau) : sand.smp@gouv.nc

Bibliographie

ANDERSON, A. & CLARK, G., 1999, The age of Lapita settlement in Fiji. *Archaeology in Oceania* 34, p. 31-39.

BALOUET, J.C. & OLSON, S.L., 1989, *Fossil Birds from Late Quaternary Deposits in New Caledonia.* Smithsonean Contributions to Zoology 469. Washington D.C.: Smithsonian Institution.

BEDFORD, S., 2000, Pieces of the Vanuatu Puzzle: archaeology of the North, South and Centre. Unpublished PhD Thesis, ANU Canberra.

BURLEY, D., NELSON, D. E., & SHUTLER Jr, R., 1999. A radiocarbon chronology for the Eastern Lapita frontier in Tonga. *Archaeology in Oceania* 34, p. 59-72.

BURLEY, D. & DICKINSON, W., 2001, Origin and significance of a founding settlement in Polynesia. *Proceedings of the National Academy of Science* 98 (20), p. 11829-11831.

FRIMIGACCI, D., 1980, Localisation éco-géographique et utilisation de l'espace de quelques sites Lapita de Nouvelle-Calédonie : essai d'interprétation, *Journal de la Société des Océanistes* 66-67, p. 5-11.

FRIMIGACCI, D., 1999, Où sont allés les potiers Lapita de Bourail? Remarques sur le site WKO001. In *The Western Pacific, 5000 to 2000 B.P.: Colonisations and transformations*, édité par J.C. Galipaud et J. Lilley. Paris: ORSTOM Editions, p. 63-84.

GALIPAUD, J.C., 1996, New Caledonia: Some recent archaeological perspectives, in J. Davidson, G. Irwin, F. Leach, A. Pawley and D. Brown, eds., *Oceanic Culture History. Essays in Honour of Roger Green*. New Zealand Journal of Archaeology Special Publication, p. 297-305.

GIFFORD, E.W. & SHUTLER Jr, R., 1956, *Archaeological Excavations in New Caledonia*, Anthropological Records 18, University of California, Berkeley and Los Angeles.

GOLSON, J., 1971, Lapita Ware and its transformations. In *Studies in Oceanic Culture History Vol. 2.*, édité par R. Green et M. Kelly. Pacific Anthropological Records 12, Honolulu, p. 67-76.

GREEN, R.C., 1979, Lapita, in J. Jennings, ed., *The Prehistory of Polynesia*. Cambridge, MA: Harvard University Press, p. 27-60.

GREEN, R.C., 1991, A Reappraisal of the Dating for some Lapita Sites in the Reef Santa-Cruz Group of the South-East Solomons. *Journal of the Polynesian Society*, Vol. 100, p. 197-207.

GREEN, R.C., 1997, Linguistic, biological and cultural origins of the initial inhabitants of Remote Oceania. *New Zealand Journal of Archaeology* 17 (1995), p. 5-27.

GREEN, R.C. & KIRCH, P.V., 1997, Lapita exchange systems and their Polynesian transformations : seeking explanatory models. In *Prehistoric long-distance interaction in Oceania : an interdisciplinary approach*, édité par M.I. Weisler. New Zealand Archaeological Association Monograph 21, p. 19-37.

KIRCH, P.V., 1997, *The Lapita peoples: Ancestors of the Oceanic World*. Blackwell Publishers.

KIRCH, P.V., 2000, *On the Road of the Winds: An Archaeological History of the Pacific Islands Before European Contact*. The University of California Press, Berkeley.

KIRCH, P.V., 2001, *Lapita and its transformations in Near Oceania. Archaeological investigations in the Mussau Islands, Papua New Guinea, 1985-88* (vol. 1). University of California at Berkeley. Archaeological Research Facility, Contribution 59.

ROSS, M., PAWLEY, A., & OSMOND, M., 1998, *The lexicon of Proto Oceanic*. Canberra: Pacific Linguistics C-152.

SAND, C., 1995, *Le temps d'avant. La préhistoire de la Nouvelle-Calédonie*. Paris: L'Harmattan.

SAND, C., 1996, *Le début du peuplement austronésien de la Nouvelle-Calédonie. Données archéologiques récentes*. Nouméa : Les Cahiers de l'Archéologie en Nouvelle-Calédonie 6.

SAND, C., 1997a, The chronology of Lapita ware in New Caledonia, *Antiquity* 71, p. 539-547.

SAND, C., 1997b, *Lapita. The pottery collection from the site at Foué, New Caledonia*. Nouméa : Les Cahiers de l'Archéologie en Nouvelle-Calédonie 7.

SAND, C., 1999, Lapita and non-lapita ware during New Caledonia's first millenium of austronesian settlement. In *The Pacific from 5000 to 2000 BP. Colonisation and transformations*, édité par J.C. Galipaud et I. Lilley. Paris : IRD, p. 139-159

SAND, C., 2000a, The specificities of the "Southern Lapita Province" : the New Caledonian case. *Archaeology in Oceania* 35, p. 20-33.

SAND, C., 2000b, La datation du premier peuplement de Wallis et Futuna: contribution à la définition de la chronologie Lapita en Polynésie occidentale. *Journal de la Société des Océanistes* 111, p. 165-172.

SAND, C., 2001, Evolutions in the Lapita Cultural Complex: a view from the Southern Lapita Province. *Archaeology in Oceania* 36, p. 64–75.

SAND, C., BOLÉ, J., & OUETCHO, A., 2002, Site LPO023 of Kurin: characteristics of a Lapita settlement in the Loyalty Islands (New Caledonia). *Asian Perspectives*.

SAND, C., & SHEPPARD, P., 2000, Long distance prehistoric obsidian imports in New Caledonia: characteristics and meaning. *Comptes-rendus de l'Académie des Sciences de Paris. Sciences de la Terre et des planètes*. Vol. 331, p. 235-243.

SIORAT, J.P., 1990, A technological analysis of Lapita pottery decoration. In *Lapita Design Form and Composition*, édité par M. Spriggs, Occasional paper in Prehistory 19. Canberra: Australian National University Press, p. 59-82.

SPRIGGS, M., 1997a, *The Island Melanesians*. Blackwell, Oxford.

SUMMERHAYES, G., 2000, *Lapita Interaction*. Terra Australis 15. Research School of Pacific and Asian Studies. Australian National University, Canberra.

STRUCTURE, SPATIAL METAPHORS AND LANDSCAPE: A STUDY OF THE CEREMONIAL *MARAE* TEMPLE GROUNDS IN THE SOCIETY ISLANDS, FRENCH POLYNESIA

Paul WALLIN & Reidar SOLSVIK

Abstract: This study on ceremonial structures in the Society Island, French Polynesia, focuses on structural metaphors that can be seen in the organization of the household, the place for performances, and the place for the treatment of the dead, in relation to the organization of the ceremonial temple ground, the marae. It could be seen that the different places in general have the same basic outline which is a fenced courtyard, with a house or a platform at one short side. The second part of the paper deals with the location of the marae on the landscape. These relations have furthermore been mentioned in different ethnohistorical descriptions. In an effort to try to test the accuracy of such descriptions we carried out a Correspondence Analysis on different variables tied to the individual marae structures (the variables include architectural features, as well as different landscape features and orientations) the outcome of the analysis show that the variables on one axis is tied to coast –inland features and the other axis is tied to personal/individual factors at one end and collective/social factors on the other end. Using this analysis we hope to get clear of the fallacies of a purely structuralistic method, as well as a purely phenomenological research strategy.

Résumé: Structure, métaphores spatiales et paysage. –Une étude sur les sites de culte (marae) dans les Iles de la Société, Polynésie Française. Cette étude sur les structures de cérémonie porte sur les métaphores spatiales trouvées dans l'organisation du foyer, le lieu de spectacle et le lieu de traitement des morts, en relation avec l'organisation du site de culte marae. On a observé que ces lieux ont en général la même organisation de base, c.à.d. une enceinte avec un bâtiment ou plate-forme sur un des côtés courts. La 2ième partie de l'article concerne la localisation du marae dans le paysage. Ces relations ont également été mentionnées dans plusieurs descriptions ethnohistoriques. Mais en essayant de vérifier l'exactitude de ces descriptions nous avons fait une Analyse des Données sur plusieurs variables liées aux structures individuelles de marae (ces structures comprennent des caractéristiques architecturales et aussi différentes caractéristiques du paysage et des orientations). Le résultat de l'analyse montre que les variables d'un premier axe de l'Analyse des Données sont liées aux caractéristiques spatiales de côte/arrière-pays, et celles du deuxième axe aux facteurs personnels/individuels d'un côté et collectifs/sociaux de l'autre. En utilisant cette analyse nous espérons éviter les pièges causés par une méthode soit purement structurelle, soit purement phénoménologique.

INTRODUCTION

In this paper we will present some of our resent research on the *marae* (ceremonial sites) in the Society Islands, French Polynesia. The Society Islands are located in Central East Polynesia. The Island group is divided into the Windward Islands and the Leeward Islands (Fig. 1). Here we consider the structural organisation of habitation and ceremonial sites in the Society Islands (Cf. Kirch 1996; Kirch and Green 2001; Ladefoged 1998; Weisler & Kirch 1985:154-155), as well as relations between the *marae* and the surrounding landscape.

THE HOUSHOLD

The settlement pattern in proto-historic Tahiti is described as dispersed, and the basic unit of habitation was the household. John Turnbull, who visited Tahiti in the late 18th century, wrote: "These houses are generally surrounded with a kind of court-yard encircled with a stout ailing about three feet high ... In this yard are sheds and smaller huts" (Turnbull 1802-03:355-3x6). This area, or courtyard, of the household was enclosed by a fence termed *aumoa*. (Parkinson 1773:23; Morrison 1Xxx:197; Handy 1923:34-35; Green et al. 1967:174-175; Ferdon 1981:79), which have not been found archaeologically – so far. Within this courtyard, several houses with discreet functions were located. Generally, the household consisted of a sleeping house, *fare taoto*, usually with a paved area in front; a cook-house or *fare tutu*; garden or horticultural terraces; and a shrine for worshipping of the family god. Among the "better situated", the household in addition had a canoe house, the *farau va'a*. In fact the residence of a chief may in some instances have been used as an assembly ground, or else there was a separate assembly house, *fare apo'oraa*, for the community close by. Also, the fare heiva, a house for performance might have been co-located with the chief's house (Green et al. 1967:175).

Structural comparison between the *marae*, the sleeping house (fare taoto), the house of performance (fare heiva), and the fare tupapa'u, or death-house will be conducted. The general layout of a *marae* is a rectangular area, in the Windward Islands this was enclosed by a fence, with the *ahu*, a raised elongated stone structure, as a focal point at one end (Fig. 2). The area in front of the *ahu* was usually paved, there were wooden altars, *fata-rau*, for food-offerings (Fig. 3), and upright-stones serving as backrests for important people attending ceremonies at the *marae*. The space of the *marae* seems to have been divided into at least three zones (Henry 1928; Wallin & Solsvik n.d.). Only the priests, and on certain occasions the firstborn chief of the tribe, might approach the area in front of the *ahu*, the gods themselves occupying the top of the *ahu*. Frequently, backrests for the chief and his wife where located midway between the *ahu* and the opposite end. The rest of the participants in the ceremony were situated at the entrance end of the *marae*. Commoners and women had to stay outside. That the *marae* was perceived as the "home-

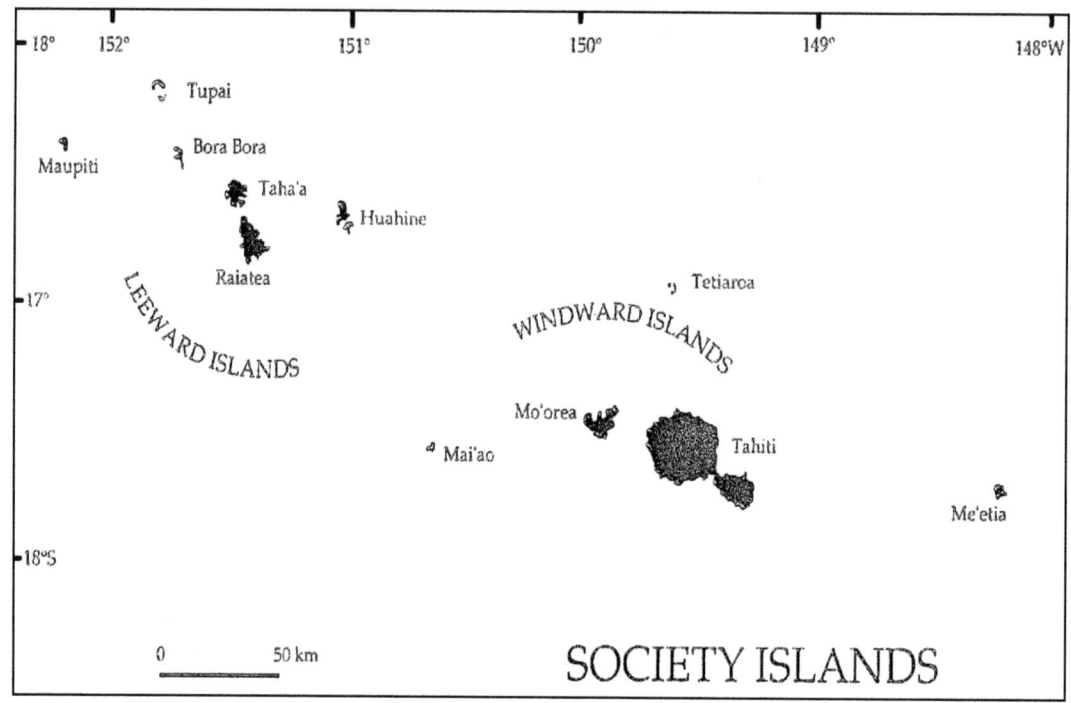

Figure 1. The Pacific Islands and the location of the Society Islands in Central Eastern Polynesia.

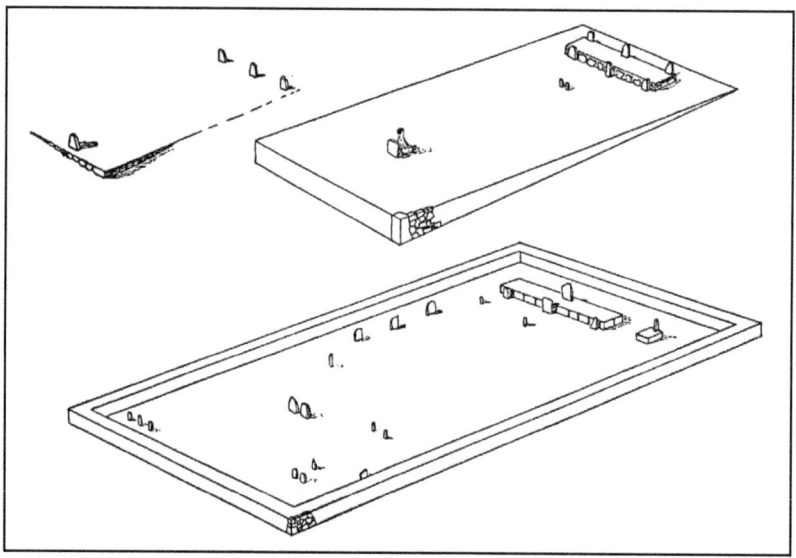

Figure 2. Schematic drawing of *marae* structures in Windward Society Islands (from Emory 1933).

of-the-god" is attested by Teitura Henry's description on the inauguration of a national *marae*. As the priest "went up into the marae", or the *ahu*, and sprinkled water, he invited the tutelar god to "take possession of his new home" (Henry 1928:137).

"This was called the rao-marae (setting of the marae). Then the young maidens returned to their post at the side, while the high priest, taking sea water in a gourd, **went up into** the marae and sprinkled it everywhere, as he called upon the tutelar god, whose name he repeated, **to take possession of his new home**, and to make welcome his guests, the hosts of gods" (Henry 1928:137) [Emphasis by us].

When the tutular god participated in the ceremonies, it was placed in the *avaa-rahi* (Henry 1928:133) directly in front of the *ahu*, and we might assume that the *ahu* symbolically represented the house-of-the-god. Then the *marae* must be the household-of-the-god.

In Sydney Parkinson's pen-and-wash drawing (Ferdon 1981:71) of a dwelling complex for a Tahitian chief, we might see this same structural pattern (Fig. 4). The Tahitian term '*marae*' (Davies1991 [1851]:133) means both "the sacred place formerly used for worship, ...", as well as "cleared of wood, weed, rubbish, as a garden, or the place of worship". The courtyard, and the inside of the sleeping house, *fare taoto*, was kept clean and either covered with

Figure 3. Human sacrifice at a marae on Tahiti during J. Cook's third visit (from Cook 1784).

Figure 4. The household of a Tahitian chief. Drawing by Sydney Parkinson (from Ferdon 1981).

grass or, as out in the courtyard, paved with stones (Banks 1774:340; Ellis 18xx:176-177; Parkinson 1773:23; Tobin 1Xxx:85-86; Cf. also Ferdon 1981:80). The many altars for food-offerings located at various places at the *marae*, can be compared to the racks for hanging raw food outside in the courtyard (Ferdon 1981:81-82; Cf. also pen-and-wash drawing by S. Parkinson, p. 77, Ferdon 1981) or inside the cookhouse (Handy 1932:24).

During the survey of various structures in the 'Opunohu valley on Mo'orea, Green and his colleagues excavated a couple of chiefs or assembly houses with a possible fare heiva in connection to it (Green *et al*. 1967:164-170 & 174-176). As we can see, the main house is a chief's house with a paved rectangular court in front of it. At one end of the court there is what most probably is a fare heiva (Green *et. al*. 1967:165, fig. 16). Instead of having the two structures separate, they in this case make up one integrated structure, as sometimes *marae*-complexes also contains additional structures (Cf. de Bovis 1980:45; Wallin 1993: 34-35, 1998:12-14).

Looking at the fare heiva (Fig. 5) depicted by John Webber (Ferdon 1981:13 1) from Tahiti in 1776, one cannot escape the feeling that in very general terms the structure resembles that of a *marae*. The enclosed space has a raised building at one end, which may suggest the symbolical similarity to the walls, the court, and *ahu* of the *marae*. From the front of the house, extending a bit out on the court there is mats, instead of the paved area in front of the *ahu*. As in the *marae*, the ceremony, or the dance is being conducted on this "paved" area, while the general crowds are outside the parameters of the structure (Cf. de Bovis 1980:44 & 50-51; Henry 1928:125, 137-138, 166, 170, and 175). Henry (1928:133) also states that the drums were situated almost at the centre of the *marae*, near one of the short-ends, as the drums in the drawing. The same structural principles seem to be used in the *fare tupapa'u*, illustrated by John Webber (Ferdon 1981:16 1) (Fig. 6).

THE MARAE IN THE LANDSCAPE

Natural elements, such as, sea (water), land, and sky, were central in Polynesian creation myths. Therefore such elements played a central role in their world-view. In Tahitian creation myths we can find words like: "The universe was in darkness with water everywhere" (Handy 1927:14) or "the gods were born in the confined sky" (ibid. 1927:16). The sky and earth was furthermore separated by

Figure 5. A Tahitian fare heiva, or house for performances. Depicted by John Webber (from Ferdon 1981).

Figure 6. A fare tupapa'u or death house. Depicted by John Webber (from Ferdon 1981).

the creating god Ta'aroa (Henry 1928:337). After that, the growth of land continued, and nature was described in Tahitian myths like: "The growth of the mountains, the growth of the streams, the growth of the sea, the growth of the coral, the growth of the heavens etc" (Handy 1927:18). These connection of the natural elements, and the stories of creation gave of course meanings to the landscape, meanings that were of importance when selecting the building place of the *marae*. The landscape was closely related to the gods who were the creators, and the *marae* were built in honour of the gods.

Landmarks such as projecting points, passages in the coral reef, and mountain peaks, created by the gods, were certainly of great importance when it came to the localisation of the ceremonial sites. Teutira Henry is also connecting the location of *marae* to the three main social groups, namely the "royal" ari'i chief group, the "gentlemen" or ra'atira, and finally the "common people" called the manahune, she writes: "Upon the prominent points were the royal *marae*; in the bays were the gentlemen's *marae*; and behind them were the *marae* of the common people" (Henry 1928:150).

The environmental elements are in short the following: 1) *The sea*, including the open ocean, the coral reef section, and the lagoon. 2) *The land*, including the beach area, the coastal plain, and the valley. Locating elements within these main areas are projecting points, mountain ridges and peaks, as well as sweet water resources, such as river systems, waterfalls, pools and lakes. 3) *The sky*, including the sun, the moon, and stars, as well as geographical directions (N, S, E, W).

The open sea was of course important as provider of main food resources, and was also an ocean of legendary seafarers, with stories such as: "After Rû and Hina had located lands, Mâ-û-i and his flotilla sailed again over the ocean, for his king, Ama-tai-atea (Outrigger-of-the-expansive-ocean). As he and his people arrived at lands, they built temples conveniently and assigned them to priests" (Henry 1928:464). The sea was of course the link for

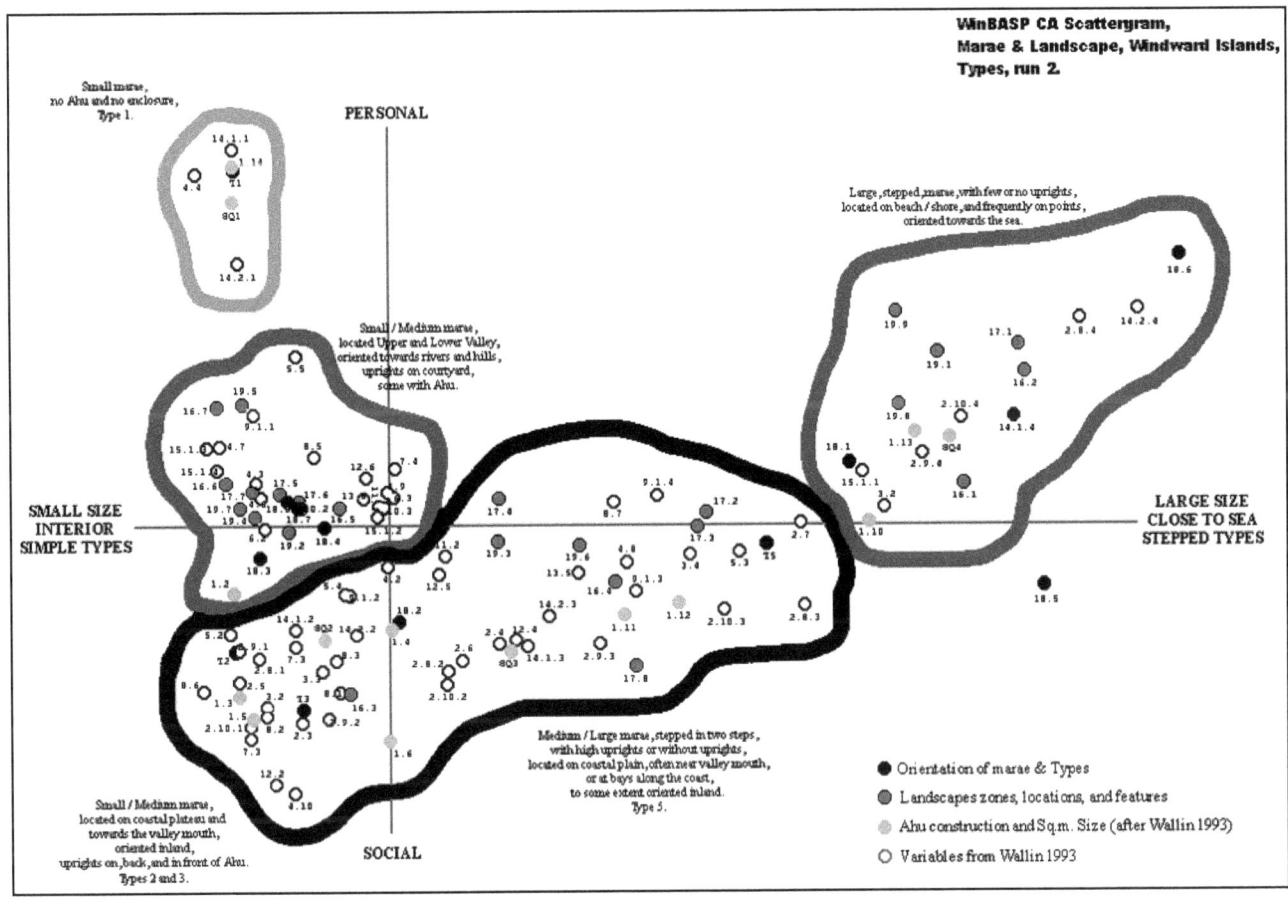

Figure 7. The Correspondence Analysis of construction and landscape variables tied to the marae in the Windward Society Islands.

communications between islands, as well as the domain of the fishermen catching the big game of pelagic fish, dolphins and sea-turtles, that was high status foods for the ari'i chiefs (Henry 1928:381). The passage in the coral reef was also of great importance. This was the entrance to the sea and the (is)land. For example, the passage in the reef at the great *marae* Taputapuatea at Opoa on Raiatea was called Te-ava-moa, which means "The sacred passage" (Henry 1928:120). The calm waters of the lagoon, was also full of small fish, and access to water in general was of great importance in different *marae* rituals, Henry mentions that "the *marae* was cleared and sprinkled well by the priests with sea water to make it holy" (Henry 1928:132).

The location of the *marae* close to the lagoon side may indicate its relation to this natural element (some of these structures may also have been dedicated to the fishermen or the canoe builders in the area), but if there is a passage in the reef close to the *marae*, this might indicate that the access to the open sea was important. It indicates that the *marae* was accessible for visitors from far and near. Such main structures may have been of importance on the external political arena, a focal point for visitors. The *marae* built at the beach region or at projecting points is probably in some way dedicated to the sea or the external world.

The coastal plain was a very fertile area with intensive agricultural and plantation activities. If the *marae* was located in this area it might have been associated with such activities. The coastal plain was also an extensive living area. The ownership of the land was of importance to show. The *marae* was used when claiming the rights to certain land areas (Henry 1928:141-142). The coastal plain may be seen as the main internal political arena, in the competition between families, lineages and district groups.

The valleys extended about 10-15 km inland. The main river, and its smaller connecting river arms was the main localisation factors for *marae* structures inside the valleys, as well as waterfalls coming down the steep valley sides, because of the importance of the water in cleaning rituals before and after *marae* ceremonies (Handy 1927:52). Terraced taro plantations, and certain wild resources such as, fei bananas and bamboo (ofe) might also have been of importance for the location of certain specialised structures. These structures were probably of interest at the local political arena when it comes to the control over certain resources valuable for the people of the valley and connecting coastal plain.

Descriptions above were mainly based on ethnohistorical descriptions of *marae* structures and their theoretical location on the landscape. So, one can really ask; what picture may be shown through archaeological practice? The diagram (Fig. 7) show the preliminary results of a statistical Correspondence Analysis based on construction variables defined in the PhD thesis by P. Wallin (1993), with some new landscape oriented variables added. The horizontal axis shows landscape, size and type orientation, and the vertical axis show social aspects.

The right field represents large stepped *marae* located on the beach/shore, with an orientation towards the sea/opening of the reef. They were the expression of certain individuals/high chiefs as an externally oriented power demonstration. The big central field represents a mixed group of *marae* located on the coastal plain/ridges and lower valley, where the *ahu* generally is oriented towards the interior. These structures had a social/tribal function, used in land division and internal power struggles. The two left fields represents medium and small *marae* located up the valley. The *ahu* (when existing) was oriented towards rivers and hills. These *marae* also represented specialized structures with more limited functions directed towards specific individuals.

In summary this statistical analysis is in line with the ethnohistorical descriptions, which in individual cases points at the fact that large coastal-bound structures were tied to powerful individuals, and that medium/lesser structures on the coastal plain or located further inland were tied to the lineage/family group or specialists.

Authors' Address

Paul WALLIN
Reidar SOLSVIK
The Kon-Tiki Museum
Institute for Pacific Archaeology and Cultural History
Bygdøynesveien 36, 0286 Oslo, NORWAY

Bibliography

BANKS, J., 1896. Journal of the Right Hon. Sir Joseph Banks, during Captain Cook's first voyage. London.

DE BOVIS, E., 1980. *Tahitian Society before the arrival of the Europeans*. Translation and Introduction by R.D. Craig. 2nd ed. Brigham Young University, Laie, Hawaii.

COOK, J., 1784. *Cook's Voyage to the Pacific Ocean* Vol. II. John Stocksdale, London.

DAVIES, J., 1991. *A Tahitian and English Dictionary with Introductory Remarks on the Polynesian Language and a Short Grammar of the Tahitian Dialect: with an appendix.* Originally printed in 1851, at the London Missionary Society's Press, Papeete, Tahiti. (Facsimile 1991 edition, Papeete, Haere Po No Tahiti.

ELLIS, W., 1830. *Polynesian Researches*. Vol. 1. London.

EMORY, K.P., 1933: *Stone Remains in the Society Islands*. B. P. Bishop Mus. Bull. 116. Honolulu.

FERDON, E.N., 1981. *Early Tahiti as the Explorers Saw it; 1767-1797*. Tucson.

GREEN, R.C., GREEN, K., RAPPAPORT, R.A., RAPPAPORT, A. & DAVIDSON, J., 1967. Archaeology on the Island of Mo'orea, French Polynesia. *Anthropological Papers of the American Museum of Natural History 51(2)*. New York.

HANDY, E.S.C., 1923. *The Native Culture in the Marquesas*. B.P. Bishop Museum Bulletin 9 / Bayard Dominick Expedition Publication Number 9, B.P. Bishop Museum Press, Honolulu,

HANDY, E.S.C., 1927. *Polynesian Religion*. B. P. Bishop Mus. Bull. 34. Honolulu.

HANDY, E.S.C., 1932. *Houses, Boats, and Fishing in the Society Islands*. Bernice P. Bishop Museum Bulletin 90.

HENRY, T., 1928. *Ancient Tahiti*. Bernice P. Bishop Museum Bulletin 48. Honolulu.

KIRCH P. V., 1996. Tikopia Social Space Revisited. In: '*Oceanic Culture History. Essays in Honour of Roger Green*', pp. 257-274, Eds.: Janet Davidson, Geoffrey Irwin, Foss Leach, Andrew Pawley and Dorothy Brown, New Zealand Journal of Archaeology Special Publication 1996.

KIRCH, P. V. & R. C. GREEN, 2001. Hawaiki'i homeland...

LADEFOGED, THEGN N., 1998. Spatial Similarities and Change in Hawaiian Architecture: The Expression of Ritual Offering and Kapu in Luakini Heiau, Residential Complexes, and Houses, *Asian Perspectives*, Vol. 37, No. 1, pp. 59-73, Hawaiian University Press, Honolulu.

MORRISON, J., 1935. *The Journal of James Morrison, Boatswain's mate of the Bounty, Describing the Mutiny and Misfortunes of the Mutineers, Together with an Account of the Island of Tahiti*. O. Rutter (ed.). London.

PARKINSON, S., 1773. *Journal of a Voyage to the South Seas*. London.

SINOTO, Y. H., 1996: Mata'ire'a Hill, Huahine: A unique prehistoric settlement, and a hypothetical sequence of *marae* development in the Society Islands. In: *Oceanic Culture History. Essayes in Honour of Roger Green*. Eds: J. Davidson et. al.. New Zealand Journal of Archaeology Special Publication.

TURNBULL, J., 1813. A voyage around the world in the years 1800-1804. London.

WALLIN, P., 1993: *Ceremonial Stone Structures. The Archaeology and Ethnohistory of the Marae Complex in the Society Islands, French Polynesia*. Ph.D. diss. Uppsala University. Aun 18. Uppsala.

WALLIN, P. & R. SOLSVIK, n.d. Conceptual origin of the east Polynesian *marae*: a speculative, historical, and structural essay.

WEISLER, M. & P. V. KIRCH, 1985. The Structure of Settlement Space in a Polynesian Chiefdom: *Kawela*, Molokai, Hawaiian Islands', New Zealand Journal of Archaeology, Vol. 7, pp.129-158.

AN EARLY IRON AGE POPULATION SETTLEMENT SYSTEM IN WESTERN SIBERIA

Natalia MATVEEVA

Abstract: People of the Early Iron Age of Western Siberia worked out ways to adapt life-support systems to changing conditions. The Sargatka culture population was the most developed in socio-economic relations. Concentrations of sites around fortresses, outposts of territorial development suggest settlement by sister-type communities. In the limits of a micro region, the situation of the different functioning settlements shows the organization of economic life, hierarchical construction and localization of necropolis–land tenure between family groups. The simple settlements consist of circle or lined planning of dwellings. They were inhabited by the minimal unit of 5–6 households, making a dispersed community. The bigger units were based in fortresses with their agricultural surroundings; they were structured in many ethnic groups of different social status. Economic modeling on the materials of different types of settlements shows that there was a combination of half-nomadic, half-settled, nomadic and settled economic-cultural types in regional and social groups of the population with the formation of subcultures as a result. Systematic distribution of fortresses in the area, according to a plan in the situation of defense posts along the boundaries, and division into centres of first and second order, show the hierarchical system of settlement and the considerable centralization of management.

The ancient societies of the Early Iron Age of the forest-steppe zone of Western Siberia worked out ways to adapt life-support systems to changing natural and social-political conditions; by the use of social-normative regulators, they created an optimal combination of economic forms and social structures. The Sargatka culture population was the most developed in socio-economic relations. They occupied almost the entire south of Western Siberia. The culture existed almost a thousand years: from the 5th century BC to the 5th century AD.

In the forest-steppe, the archaeological sites of Sargatka culture numerously dominate over those of other periods - there are about 600 of them (fig. 1). The majority of sites are represented by kurgans, but there are fewer fortresses. The ratio between the number of fortresses and number of settlements equates to 1: 6.5. According to the concentration of sites in the Irtysh-basin, 40% of all sites, this was the centre of the Sargarka culture territory. The monotonous simple circle and lined planning of settlements and small number of houses-dwellings show that they were inhabited by the minimal social-economic unit of 5 or 6 households, making a dispersed community. The bigger social–economic units were based in ancient fortresses with their agricultural surroundings; they were structured in many ethnic groups of different social and property status. Fortresses are situated by chain on the boundaries of the Sargatka culture territory from the north, west and east, as mentioned by L.N. Koryakova [Корякова, 1988]. The castles' square varies considerably: from 1-2 hectares to 6 hectares, including villages beyond the defensive lines. The sizes of fortified places in Sargatka fortresses were not big, on average 100 x 100 m, and usually did not have large surrounding settlements. The biggest are the Rafailovo fortress in the Transurals and Batakovo in the Irtysh-basin (fig. 2).

Long-term use of the fortress could be conditioned by its profitable strategic and economic situation and establishment of a bigger territory with different arable lands near riverside roads. As an example, the Rafailovo settlement is situated on the fairly low zone of the first super flood-lands terrace, in the centre of spacious water-meadows. The cultural layer in the limits of fortifications is quite thick and saturated with artefacts, and is characterized by dense building. It reflects long-term use of the square that, in general, testifies to the definitely settled life of the population (fig. 5).

The Early Iron Age population planned complex building with the use of all architectural achievements already known for building wood-ground defensive constructions. There are different wooden walls: paling, palisade, closet; building of breastworks, scarping of the slopes for making them impregnable, appearance of echelon defence, footbridges, circle defence on the open place. It is a testimony of highly developed fortification building and art of war of the population and of a big role of war in their life.

A support of the study of the settlement system of tribes of the Sargatka culture are more than 20 site excavations undertaken at different times, some of which are considerable in size, up to a quarter hectare in area.

As a result, we can single out; according to the time of occupation, constant settlements and seasonal ones out, according to the elements of structure - simply and complexly structured; according to the social significance - common settlements of family-related collectives and support centres of territory development and exploration. The correlation of the different types of settlements cannot be truly determined at the present time, because the portion of explored sites out of the whole number of known ones is very small.

We consider those settlements to be inhabited constantly or over the long-term, with a cultural layer nearly 1 m thick, from 15 to 20 buildings of renewing or reconstruction of

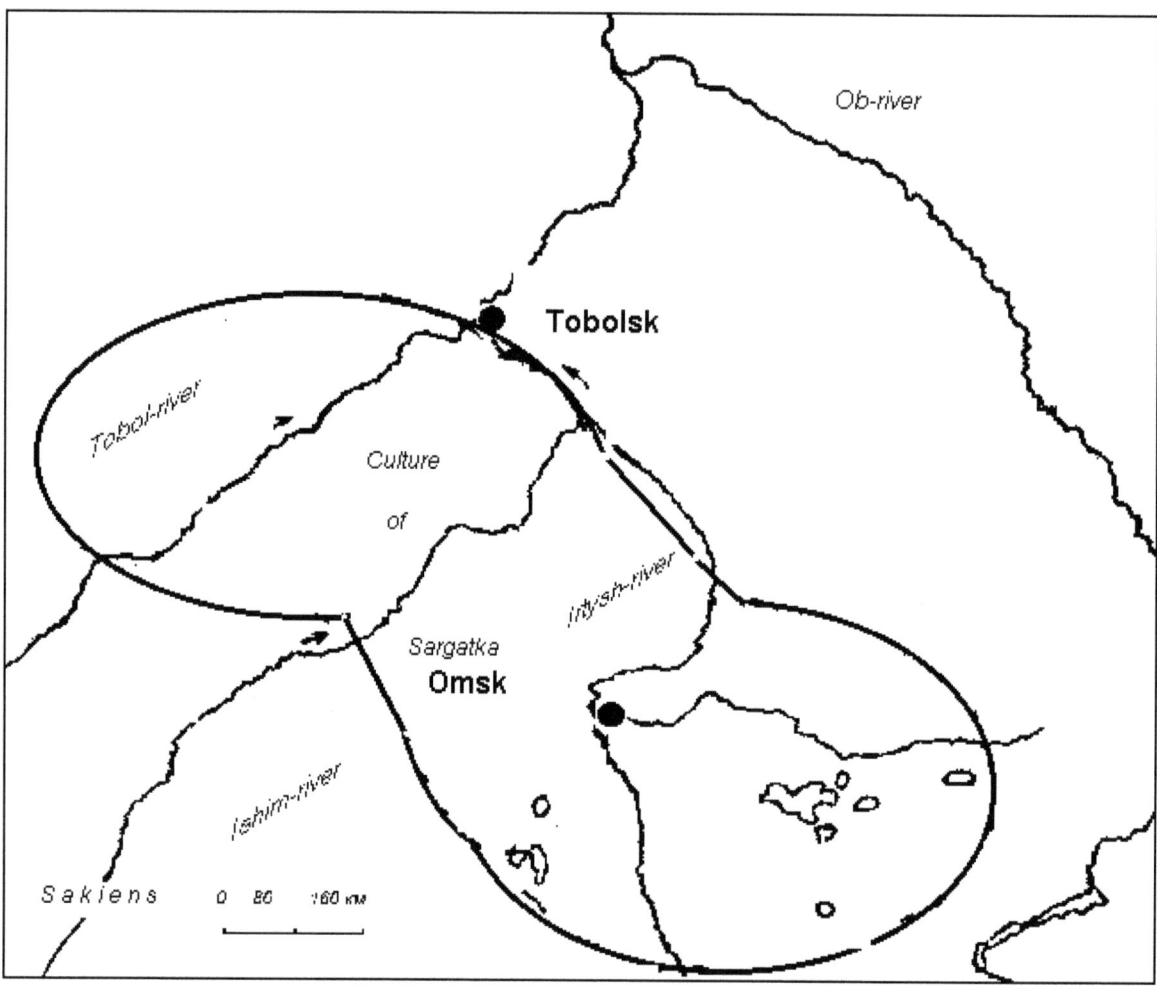

Figure 1. Map of the Western Siberia forest-steppe Sargatka culture.

dwellings, or there was a re-planning of living quarters. Saturation with trash and kitchen refuse shows the use of the square for several years or even decades. As a rule, settlements of this type are situated on waterside terraces or high remains, they are characterized by buildings of farmstead type. There are several sites similar to the constant settlements in big square, farmstead character of houses, but with a thin cultural layer and lacking repair-remains. These are Onufrievsky Borok-3, Nizhniy-Ingal-3, Ingalinka-1 etc. Probably they were left after several years because of exhaustion of the adjoining territory.

Seasonal settlements are inconsiderably smaller in area, they occupy water meadow islands, have from 5 till 10 buildings. Cultural layer is badly saturated with organic and finds, there is no house reconstruction tracks. Several sites were the stands for fishing and hunting on water-fowl. The majority of settlements have simple pile-nest or lined planning, independently from the square and time of existence. To the complexly structured sites belongs the fortress with adjoining settlements.

Rafailovo fortress presents the structure with its two fortified squares, large settlement with farmstead buildings in nest principle, new villages on the dunes in 300 m with the tracks of eight constructions, and several necropolises on surrounding heights. Kolovo fortress is also complexly structured with two defensive lines over cape, that make two squares, one of which is a citadel, four settlements on neighbouring parts of the terrace and seasonal stands in the water meadow across the river. It is also surrounded by several outstanding necropolises. The same type structures are connected with Batakovo and Bogdanovo fortresses (fig. 3).

According to the construction of sites, archaeological micro-regions can be identified. L.N. Koryakova concluded that Sargatka culture settlements on the right bank of Irtysh are situated every 8 km. In our data from the Ishym-basin, they focus on the left bank along the main waterway with the same interval. In the northern forest-steppe, in the Tobol-basin, Sargatka cultures settlements are found every 8-10 km, and necropolises every 3-4 km.

Intervals between fortresses change in the limit of 32-52 km and middle distance exhibits 40 km (fig. 4). The site and barrows concentration is more clearly manifested around fortress as a centre. For example, in the Kartashovo micro-region, there are 20 sites discovered, which spread out by a 16-17 km radius from the Kartashovo-3 fortress. We suppose that each of the fortresses, including Kartashovo-4 and Kartashovo-6, which are located much more to the south of the probational centre, was defined at some stage of this economic zone exploitation. In our

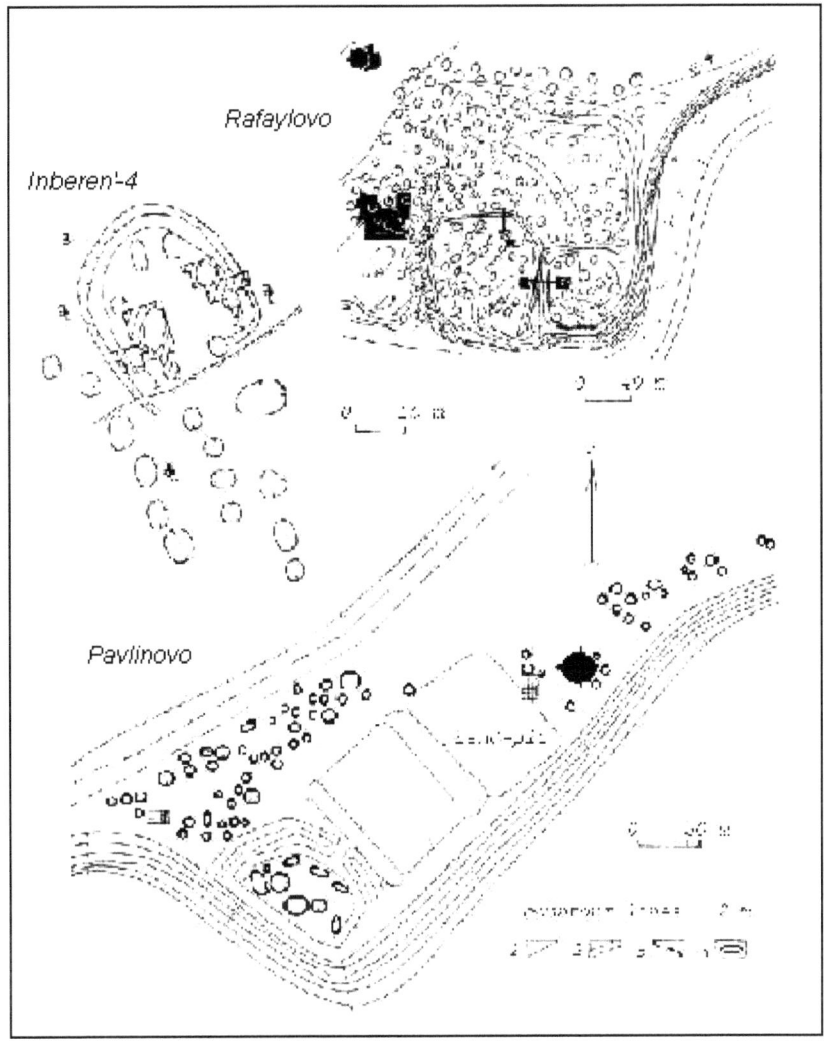

Figure 2. Plans of Sargatka culture fortresses.

view, it follows that land-tenure boundaries of that group of settlers changed over time.

The economic zone of the Batakovo micro-region, to draw it as a circle, seems bigger than that of other sites' micro-regions – 50-52 km in diameter. This fact is conformed by the large sites' compactness and number of fortresses on this territory. The Batakovo is one of the most researched Sargatka culture micro-regions in the Irtysh-basin. There are 55 sites with probational centre on the left bank river as Batakovo fortress here (Fig. 7) although it belongs to the late period of Sargatka culture. Early fortress Inberen'-4, dating IV-II centuries BC and not defined by dating fortress Stariy Karasuk-21 were situated near it. The Bogdanovo fortress on the right bank river is found near the outskirts of the circle. Its date is not clear, but it better conforms to the time of the appearance of the early necropolis Bogdanovo near it, whose chronology was defined as the 5th-4th centuries BC.

Other interpretations are impossible to make for the remaining localization scheme in this micro-region. Maybe they are like two ellipses on the left bank and on the right bank separately. The smaller area of such potential economic zones could be explained by their higher productivity (fig. 7). Our hypothesis will later be verified by local details research of burial customs in this micro-region. At present, some cranium arguments are in its support. The materials of Isakovka and Bogdanovo necropolises show that they belong to the same population group.

This zone's specialty is the maximum width of the Irtysh valley, nearly 16 km, which well provides exceptionally profitable and stable connections for complex house-keeping, with cattle-raising predominant. These reasons explain the large site concentration in the Batakovo fortresses area. We think there was high population concentration in antiquity, it shows lead situation of the same local group in the Irtysh-basin. Other arguments are the disposition series of elite necropolises from huge barrows on the hill on the right bank of the area.

Necropolises were usually founded 2-3 km from the settlement, making several kurgans around one settlement (fig. 5). Large kurgan necropolises concentrate on the highest parts of the terraces and eminences, usually on open areas with a valley view, as though they expressed a supremacy idea over the territory. As we see, the hierarchical idea of the society is expressed not only in the

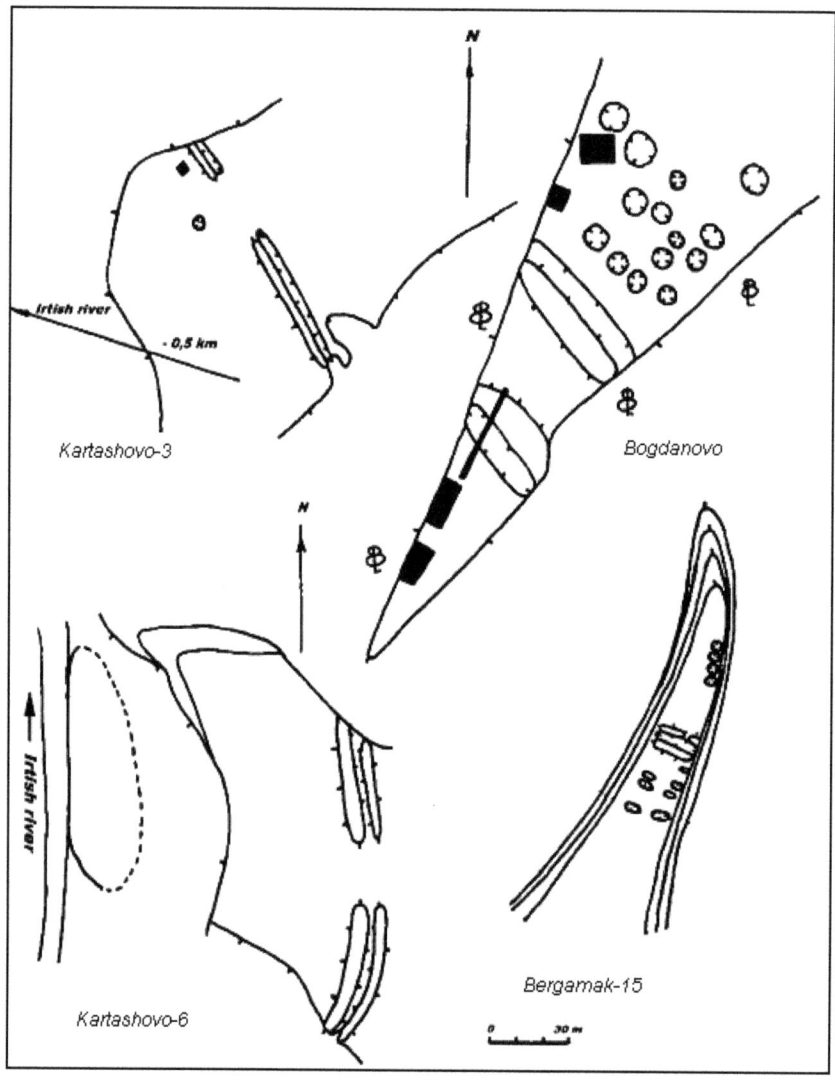

Figure 3. Plans of Sargatka culture fortresses in the Irtysh-basin.

funeral rite structure, but also in the situation of necropolises on the territory. Let's suppose that this special situation reflects the order of arable land use, traditionally fixed after separate family-related groups.

Outstanding is a systematic character in the situation of defence centre in the Sargatka culture territory: along the boundaries of the area, as long as the main waterways with one interval of 35-40 km, that shows

the definite centralization of management and warfare. Some analogies to defensive systems of the Sargatka culture region can be found in Khorezm, where the state boundaries are defended by castles from nomads. Such character of localization sites is alike to the organization of the Scythes.

In the southern forest-steppe the occupation of the tribes of the Sargatka culture was scattered, characterized mostly by short-term settlements in the northern part, and long-lived, denser population, that shows the northern forest-steppe as the main territory of their staple occupation. The western part of the area was a frontier territory with the half nomadic population of the Gorokhovo culture, on the south-west side they neighboured the summer stands of the South Urals nomads.

In the Transurals for Rafailovo micro-regions example, we find evidence of considerable climate and environmental change and related changes in the house-keeping character and duration of occupation in the fortress [Матвеева, Ларин, 2000]. This lets us make assumptions of the existence of substantial periodic land-tenure crises, which could be solved in the following ways: pasture repartition by capture of lands, passage to nomadic life of separate group of people, passage to sedentary life, hay storing for winter, etc. Then it would be logical to explain the high grade of militarization of the population by competition for resources between territorial groups. Paleoecological and paleoeconomic modeling on the materials of different types of settlements shows that there was a combination of half-nomadic, half-settled, nomadic and settled economic-cultural types in different regional and social groups of population with the formation of subcultures as a result.

A concentration of sites around the ancient settlements, outposts of territory development on equal parts of river valleys or large lake systems and existence of small non-

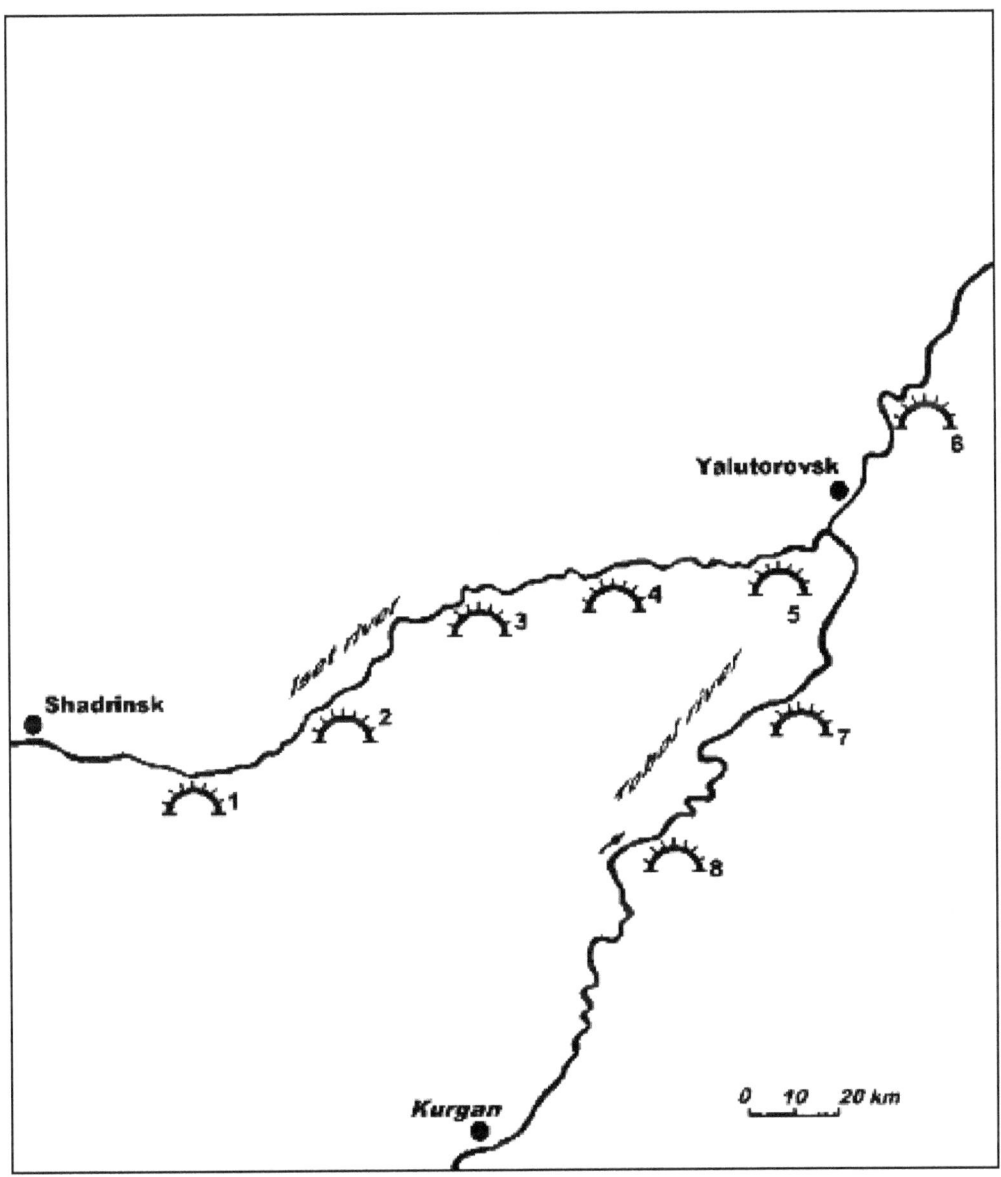

Figure 4. Situation of fortified settlements in the Tobol-basin.

developed territories on their boundaries make to conjecture the settlement by some sister type in structure and number communities. In the limits of a micro-region, the situation of the settlements with different functions shows the organization of their separate economic life, localization of necropolis and settlements in the country – organized land tenure, traditionally secured after family related groups. The hierarchical construction and situation of necropolises, insertion of them into a memorial structure of the elite cult places a functioning of the burial vault's public and sacred centres of definite ethnic-social organism.

Different types of settlements reflect the heterogeneity of the population, conditioned by the division of labour. The main part of the population was busy with housekeeping; the prosperous population held an active exchange of excess of their labour production for metal goods, ore, bars, armaments and items of personal use with neighbours for the purpose of realization of their social status in clothing and bijouterie. Unity of fashion for clothes, jewellery, instruments of production and armament on the whole territory of Sargatka culture community testifies to intensive inner cultural exchange. The elite, who needed status expression via large luxury, was especially interested in regular exchange that promoted the appearance in the 3rd century BC of constant caravan tradeways with increasing intensity of movement and submission to its purposes of depending population in distant territories and inclusion of them in the system of a Great Silk Way.

Among the variants of the distribution system's interpretation in the area of Sargatka culture settlements, one can be connected with the strengthening of settling of society elite and making of exploitation system of the own and neighbouring tribes in which the settlements were the centres of ethnic economic and political interaction, on the basis of different economic structures and cultural traditions. This has a confirmation in general line of development of fortification building with the development of early states in ancient settled agricultural and cattle-breeding-agricultural societies.

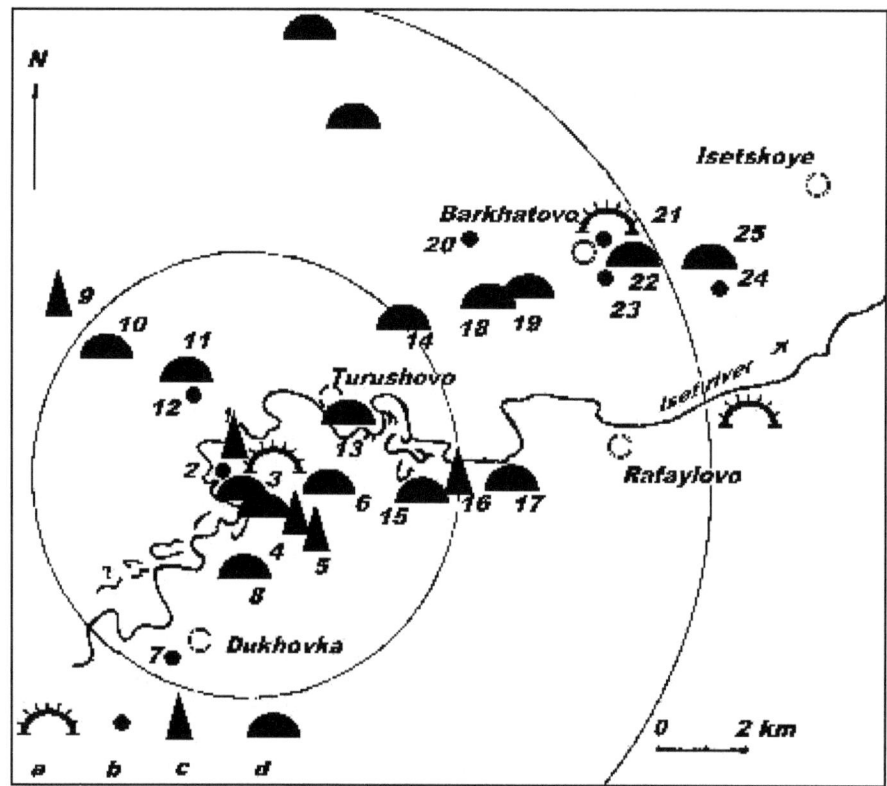

Figure 5. Potential economic zone of the Rafaylovo fortified settlement.
Legend: a- fortress, b- settlement, c- season site, d- kurgan necropoles.

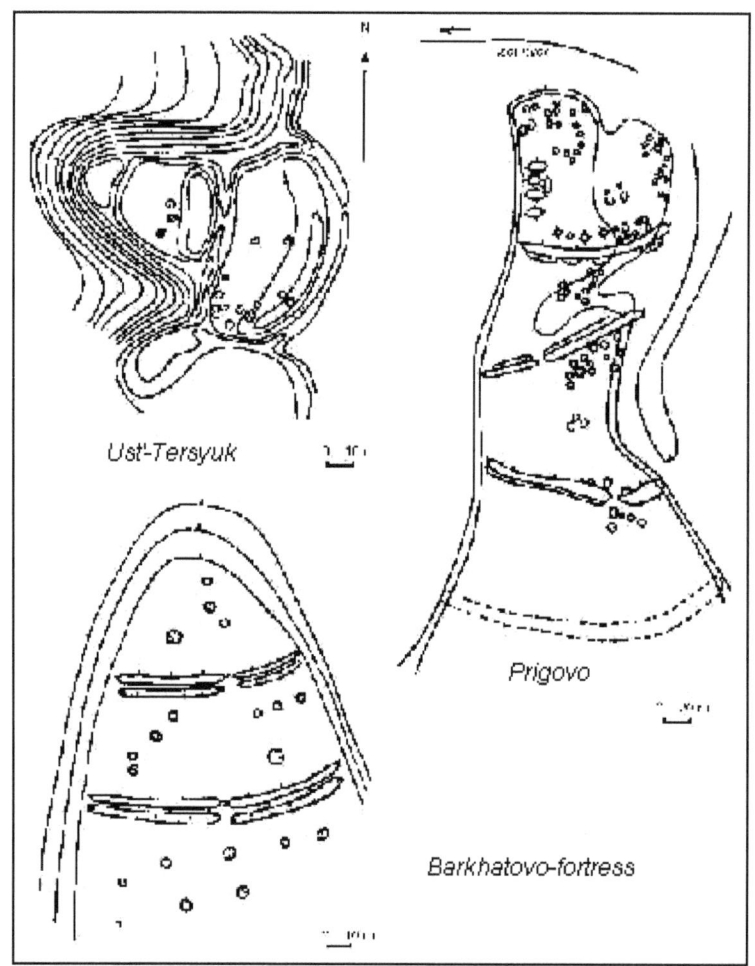

Figure 6. Plans of Sargatka culture fortified settlements in the Tobol-basin.

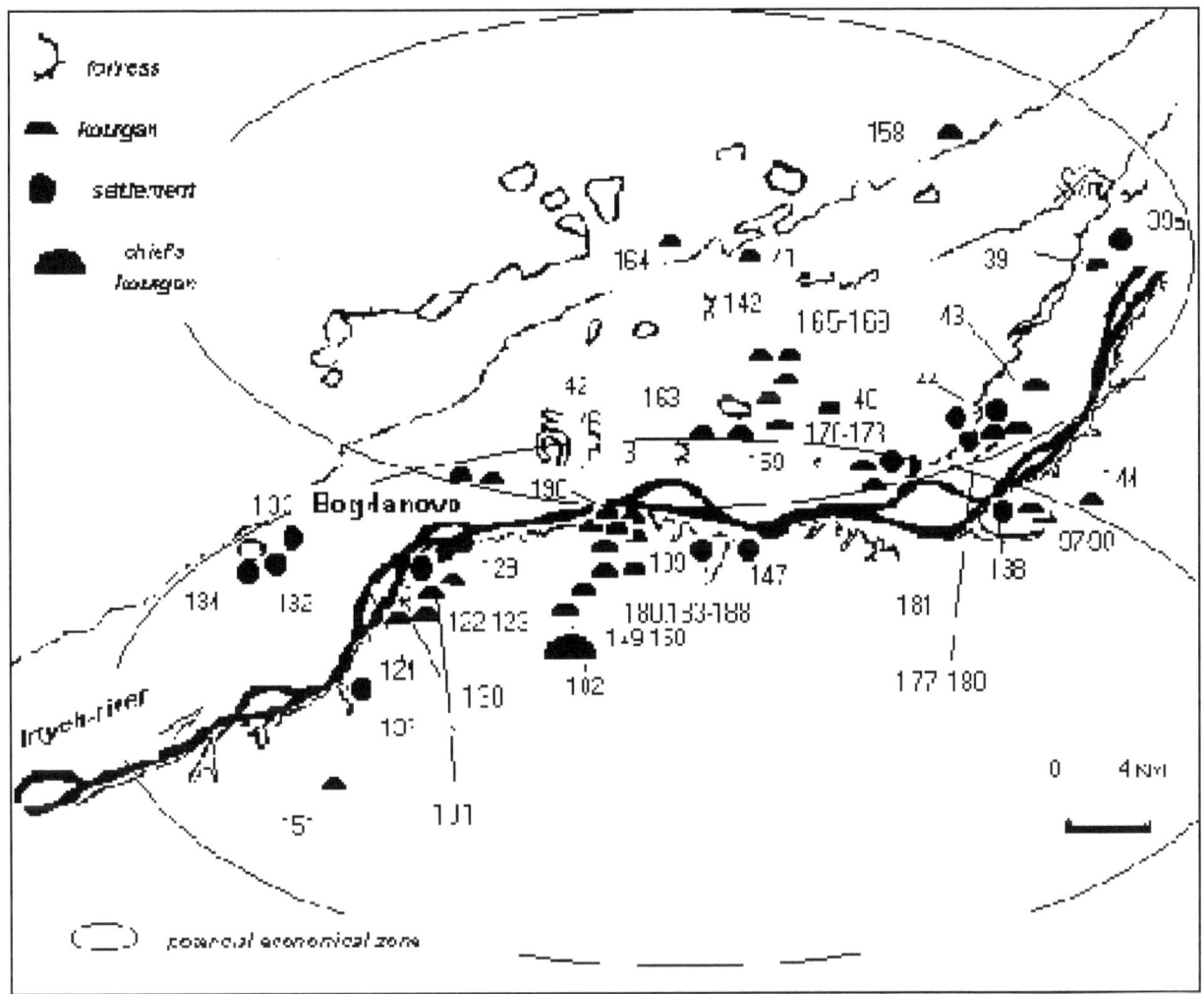

Figure 7. Potential economic zones of the Batakovo fortress.

The basic form of social communities of Early Iron Age population was a common. The lowest level was made by seasonal producing groups. The common could be of different level and consisted of many related groups. As we see, in West Siberian materials of the Early Iron Age there was an origin of social phenomena already, that further became characteristic for nomads and half nomads of Medieval Ages and Modern History. The one group dominated over others; this was the base of power organization. Also there was a community concentration in larger associations (tribes) in marginal zones and centralized unions during the periods of military concentration.

Heterogeneity of the society became apparent in different localization, square and lay-out of houses, specialties of fortification. This was expressed in building of settlements; that gives a basis to perceive an occupation by different status families, to interpret the fortresses as many-functional: avant-posts of opening of territories up and paying the tributes, refuges, chief residences, centres of territorial units. In the scale of trade development there is an indicator of a private appropriation of material welfare.

Sargatka culture society made a step in social stratification and territorial management organization in their micro-regions comparing with the beginning of the Early Iron Age. However a lined principle of situation of ancient settlements shows the lack of strict centralization of management in the limits of Sargatka culture community in general.

Author's Address

Natalia MATVEEVA
625003, box 2774
Department of archeology
Institute of Northern development of Russian Academy of Sciences
Tyumen, RUSSIA

Bibliography

MATVEEVA N.P. 1999. Some interpretation models of Sargatka culture fortresses of Western Siberia // *Complex societies of Eurasia in III-I milleniums BC*: International conference. Chelyabinsk - Arkaim, p.226-230.

MATVEEVA N.P., N.Ye. RYABIGINA. 2001 Reconstruction of Natural Conditions in the Trans-Urals in the Early Iron Age // *XIV International Congress of Prehistoric and protohistoric sciences*. 2-8 september. Liege-Belgium. Pre-prints, p.86.

www.ingramcontent.com/pod-product-compliance
Ingram Content Group UK Ltd.
Pitfield, Milton Keynes, MK11 3LW, UK
UKHW061213180426
11947UKWH00029B/2031